THE REAL SATAN

To Richard Shaw —
All Best Wishes.
Jim Kelle

THE REAL SATAN

From Biblical Times
to the Present

JAMES KALLAS

FORTRESS PRESS
MINNEAPOLIS

THE REAL SATAN
From Biblical Times to the Present

Fortress Press ex libris publication 2006

Copyright © 1975, 2006 Fortress Press, an imprint of Augsburg Fortress. All rights reserved. Except for brief quotations in critical articles or reviews, no part of this book may be reproduced in any manner without prior written permission from the publisher.
Visit http://www.augsburgfortress.org/copyrights/contact.asp or write to Permissions, Augsburg Fortress, Box 1209, Minneapolis, MN 55440.

Biblical quotations unless otherwise noted are from the Common Bible, copyright © 1973 by the Division of Christian Education of the National Council of Churches of Christ in the United States of America.

Cover art: *Red of All Reds* © Paul Fonfara
Cover design: Josh Messner

ISBN 0-8066-1466-8
The Library of Congress has catalogued the original publication as follows: Library of Congress Catalog Card Number 74–14184

The paper used in this publication meets the minimum requirements of American National Standard for Information Sciences—Permanence of Paper for Printed Library Materials, ANSIZ329.48–1984.

Manufactured in the U.S.A.

Contents

Introduction: Giving the Devil His Due 9

I. Satan in the Old Testament 15
The Heavenly Council
Transcendence and Immanence
Angels
Satan the Servant

II. Satan in the Intertestamental Period 27
Alexander the Great
Antiochus Epiphanes—Persecution
Pharisees and Sadducees
The Essenes
The Principle of Retribution
Satan—From Servant to Enemy
The Will of God
Seeds of Despair

III. Satan in the New Testament 49
The Baptism of John
The Power of Satan
New Testament Demonology

IV. Jesus in Conflict with Satan 71
Jesus' Self-understanding
The Miracles of Jesus
The Lord's Prayer
The Mission of the Disciples

V. The One Who Conquers Death 93
The Turning Point at Caesarea Philippi
To Jerusalem—and Victorious Death
Emmaus—and Understanding

Conclusion: Proclaiming God's Victory 107

Dedicated to Jacque and Jim . . .
　　　Kingsley and Paris . . .

Preface to the 2006 Publication

I am pleased that Augsburg Fortress is reprinting this book. I thank them for their thoughtfulness and commend them on their wisdom. It is good that this work is back in print. The closing chapters are profound and powerful affirmations of the compassion of Jesus and the sovereignty of God, motifs sorely lacking in our secular city. Now they are heard anew.

Since the original edition appeared well over a quarter century ago, there are some anachronisms such as the mention of Katherine Kuhlmann on page 83. She crossed the Jordan a generation ago! But the thoughtful reader will see easily that the name of any current faith healer can be inserted to replace hers and the point remains the same.

In the same vein, pages 45-47 give an evaluation of the "present" prevailing climate of pessimism and the discussion ends with comments on the Viet Nam struggle and its consequence of despair. The discussion could be updated to include an accounting of the dreary, dismal, depressing tragedy of Iraq. But the point would remain the same.

If I did rewrite any of the first edition, that rewrite would be confined to the Introduction, pages 9–13. I would expand the comments on Bultmann and his demythologizing program. He was not only wrong in dismissing Satan as irrelevant. His sins were larger than that. He said his program would change only form, not the content of the New Testament.

That claim was flat out untrue. He writes that man "bears the sole responsibility for his own feeling, thinking, and willing. He is not, *as the New Testament regards him*, the victim of a strange dichotomy which exposes him to the interference of powers outside himself." The words are his, found on page 6 of *Kerygma and Myth*, but the underlining is mine. Those six underlined words make clear that his views as to man's freedom are in opposition to the New Testament. Thus was opened the door to the practice, widespread and popular today, to treat the New Testament like a scrapbook. Endorse what is popular and erase that which is politically incorrect. The primary problem today is not the interpretation of a single passage or a specific doctrine. It is the loss of Scripture as the final authority. Replacing the Reformation's call for the final authority of *sola Scriptura* (Scripture alone) in matters of faith and life is the contemporary measuring rod of human views and experiences.

One more correction must be noted. On page 26 the sentence, "The Old Testament presents Satan as an insignificant enemy," should read instead, "The Old Testament presents Satan as an insignificant *servant*."

James Kallas
August 2006
Agua Dulce, California

INTRODUCTION

Giving the Devil His Due

What a difference a decade makes! Ten years ago, fifteen years ago Satan was pronounced dead, and every theologian of any international stature was rushing forward, volunteering to be a pallbearer at the funeral. Rudolf Bultmann read the epitaph at the graveside. Solemnly he sermonized, assuring us that the death of the devil was long overdue, for he had lingered too long, and no one any longer believed in him.

Bultmann wrote:

> Now that the forces and the laws of nature have been discovered, we can no longer believe in spirits, *whether good or evil.*
>
> Sickness and the cure of disease are likewise attributable to natural causation; they are not the result of daemonic activity or of evil spells.
>
> It is impossible to use electric light and the wireless and to avail ourselves of modern medical and surgical discoveries, and at the same time to believe in the New Testament world of spirits and miracles. (*Kerygma and Myth,* New York, Harper, 1961, pp. 4-5)

That was the theological climate ten years ago. The significant thing about Bultmann's comments is that he was no John the Baptist crying alone in the wilderness. He was no lonely pioneer summoning a theological generation to shuck off the trappings of a bygone age. He did not produce the rejection of Satan, but rather he summarized a rejection which had already taken place. He did not start the process, but rather marked the close of the process. Many theologians of the day echoed and affirmed those remarks—Satan was dead, no one believed in him anymore.

No one opposed the tide, swam against the current—or, almost no one. An occasional voice of caution was raised, a red flag waved, a warning uttered. James Stewart, the famous Scottish theologian, wrote an article titled "On a Neglected Element of New Testament Theology" in which he insisted that the devil could not all that easily be despatched without damage to theological thought as a whole. William Manson took up the plea and wrote an article on the same theme, "Principalities and Powers," carrying forward the conviction that to ignore the centrality of Satan in the New Testament was to misunderstand and pervert the New Testament—that the New Testament could not be correctly grasped unless one seriously did accept the reality of the evil one. But beyond those rare and occasional voices, there was a vacuum. Satan was not so much being attacked or cast out, as he was ignored. He just didn't matter.

Being at the time still young, and therefore very brash, I took up the challenge laid down by Stewart and Manson and began to investigate their insistence that Satan was central to New Testament thought. And my studies convinced me that they were right!

My first three books, while perhaps not eloquent, were nonetheless adamant and ardent, furiously insisting with all the fire and flame of youth, that New Testament theology of the early 1960s was on the verge of spiritual bankruptcy. It had prostituted itself, it had polluted the New Testament proclamation. It had taken the robust vigorous affirmations of the gospel and watered them down into a thin soup on which no one could survive—and all because it failed to give the devil his due. I argued strenuously that by neglecting Satan every significant New Testament doctrine had either been distorted or denied. We had a false and overly optimistic view of man. We really had no clear concept of Christ as divine redeemer wrenching us free from enslaving hostile powers. We had no doctrine of the Holy Spirit, and the sacraments had lost their significance. *Every* aspect of the New Testament had been discolored and contaminated—all because of our failure to take Satan seriously.

That is the way it was ten years ago, fifteen years ago. Satan was dead. All was right with the world. There were smiles on every side.

But today! What a dramatic swing of the pendulum! Today, it is no overstatement to say that there is no topic as widely discussed, enthusiastically endorsed, and as generally recognized as true as Satan. On every side, whether popular thought of the man in the street or the sober musings of the professional churchman in the privacy of the parish, Satan has come to the fore, dominating all discussion.

There has been a veritable explosion of emphasis on the demonic, an almost universal recognition of the reality of powerful demonic celestial forces that hold us in sway and make mockery of our aspirations. Astrology is popular, seances are being held, people read horoscopes in the belief that their destiny is spelled out by the unfeeling stars and planets above who lock them up in rigid paths from which there is no escape. Suppressed by theologians of a decade ago, the belief in the reality of the demonic was only that—suppressed—and never stifled. It has erupted with a convulsive power, almost suffocating us in its shock waves. Modern man is suddenly overwhelmed. LaVey, claiming to be a priest of Satan, was on the cover of LIFE magazine. In San Francisco, a Satan wedding took place, the vows being said in the name of the devil. Thousands of people have stood in line, breaking all time box office records, to see that popular motion picture, "The Exorcist."

And the professional theologians, late as usual, are limping along at the rear, trying to catch up, at last taking Satan seriously themselves. One learned leader of the church after another suddenly finds himself filled with prophetic insight and the obligation to announce that Satan is alive again.

But that is not the basic or fundamental reason as to why I am chagrined and disturbed by the contemporary concern over the devil. If the modern expression of conviction about Satan were simply late —but correct—one could rejoice in it. But it is *not* correct! The pendulum has swung frighteningly to the other far extreme! Whereas a decade ago, Satan was being ignored and theology consequently distorted, so also today theology is being distorted! Too much is being made of Satan today! What passes itself off as a renewed biblical concern for the reality of the demonic is not biblical at all! It is a negative, pessimistic message of despair that has nothing to do with the robust biblical affirmation of the superiority of Jesus over every foe we shall ever face! It is right to give the devil his due . . . but he is not entitled to overtime! Where once we ignored the demons, now we cower in front of them, despairing, weak, and cringing, unmindful of what the New Testament *really* says about the devil and all his works and all his ways!

Modern demonology is negative, an escapist abandonment of the real world in which we find ourselves, a bailing out, a capitulation of our power, a corruption of our convictions. Modern demonology is directly contrary to the New Testament proclamation that at the name of Jesus *every* knee shall bow and *every* tongue confess, both on the earth and under the earth, that Jesus is Lord!

What we really need in our day is not the cacaphony of voices telling us that Satan is strong. What we need is to hear the New Testament affirmation that Christ is stronger! There is no despair or discouragement in the New Testament. Satan is the strong man, but Jesus has come to bind the strong man and set at liberty those who are oppressed!

The time has come to review what the Scriptures truly say—and do not say—about the devil.

1

Satan in the Old Testament

The place to begin in discussing the biblical doctrine of Satan is with the first place he is mentioned, the Old Testament.

If one would understand the role of Satan in the Old Testament, there are two words to engrain in the memory. Those two words are (1) Satan in the Old Testament is *insignificant;* and (2) Satan in the Old Testament is a *servant* of God, not an enemy but a servant.

Let's take the two words one at a time. First, *insignificant.* How many times is Satan explicitly mentioned by name in the Old Testament? And where are those places? Can you correctly answer those questions? Very few can! Most people answer, "He is mentioned in Genesis, in the temptation of Adam and Eve, the fall into sin." Wrong! Satan is *not* mentioned there! Check your Bible carefully and you will see that it is the serpent, not Satan, who tempts Adam and Eve and leads them into sin. Satan is not present! It is only later theology that identifies Satan with the tempting serpent (we will return to that idea in this chapter), but right now the significant thing to notice is that this is *not* one of the places Satan is mentioned.

He is mentioned only three times in the entire Old Testament. Only three times! And in two of those three places, 1 Chronicles 21:1 and Zechariah 3:1-2, he is only barely mentioned. There is only one passage in the entire Old Testament, Job chapter one, in which Satan is discussed in any extended fashion. In the 39 books of the Old Testament, in the history of the Jews covering almost 1500 years, there is *only one* lengthy description of Satan, Job chapter one. That is biblical fact—and that fact leads us to say that in the Old Testament the first word to remember about Satan is that he is insignificant, playing no dominant or central role.

The second word, *servant*, takes more discussion and description. The way to begin is to discuss something which at first glance might not seem related. But bear with us, we will give some background information, and then return to the subject of Satan.

The Heavenly Council

The word "monotheism" today means a belief in one *sole* God, one God, alone in celestial splendor, by himself in the heavens above. That is what the word "monotheism" means today. But that is not what the word meant to the average Jew 2000 years ago. For the Jew, God was not the *sole* celestial being but the *supreme* celestial being. Never does the Old Testament speak about God as if he were alone in the heavens. The Bible simply will not be misunderstood at that point. God is surrounded by celestial figures, literally surrounded by thousands and thousands of cosmic beings.

Satan in the Old Testament 17

"Monotheism" in the Old Testament means not one sole God but one supreme God, raised above, towering over, all the other celestial beings that surround his heavenly throne. There are so many of these figures that they are even divided into classes. There are the cherubim, the seraphim, the angels. There are so many angels that they are further subdivided into classes—there are the ordinary angels, and then there are the archangels, some of whom we even know by name, Gabriel and Michael for example. The Book of Daniel in the Old Testament, reflecting on this vast multitude of heavenly beings, insists that there are "ten thousand times ten thousand" heavenly beings present with God in his holy court (Dan. 7:10).

This fact, that the Jew of yesteryear saw God not as all alone upstairs but rather supreme upstairs, accounts for those many titles for God found in the Psalms. God is called "The Lord God Most High" or "The Lord of Hosts." He is surrounded by a host. He is higher, more powerful, ruling over all those about him.

The ancient Jew was convinced that God ruled the world. There is probably no Old Testament thought as vigorously affirmed as the belief that God rules the world. The Psalms vibrate with that idea, "The earth is the Lord's and the fulness thereof. . . ." The Old Testament begins by affirming the sovereign majesty of God. With a word he calls all things into being. God rules. He cradles the mountains in his hands, holds the seas, creates life, sustains all. God rules.

But God rules *indirectly*. He rules through this countless cluster of cosmic beings. This band of angels, of cherubim and servants, are his servants who work his will in the world of men. Psalm after psalm describe this heavenly council. And further, the Old Testament does not get all hung up on the fine points of language. Sometimes these lesser celestial beings are even called "gods." Inferior gods, lesser beings, nowhere near the might and majesty of the most high God, but still called gods. Here are a few of the passages that speak of the one high God surrounded by these lesser gods, his heavenly council:

- *Psalm 86:8* There is none like thee among the gods, O Lord, nor are there any works like thine.

- *Psalm 96:4* For the Lord is great and greatly to be praised; He is to be revered above all gods.

- *Psalm 135:5* For I know that the Lord is great, and that our Lord is above all gods.

Notice well that these verses do not deny the *existence* of other gods. What is denied is their *independence*. They are not omnipotent. They do not have the power of the one true God, Lord over Israel. Not even Elijah, in his struggle with the priests of the god Ba'al at Mount Carmel ever denied the existence of Ba'al. What he did insist on was the impotence of Ba'al! Unlike the God of the Jews, Ba'al could not act independently. He could not send fire down from heaven. Here are some more passages that speak of God as ruling over all these other celestial members of his heavenly council:

- *Psalm 82:1* God has taken his place in the divine council; in the midst of the gods he holds judgment.

- *Psalm 89:6-7* For who in the skies can be compared to the Lord? Who among the heavenly beings is like the Lord, a God feared in the

Satan in the Old Testament

council of the holy ones, great and terrible above all that are round about him?

God rules the world, but he rules it indirectly, acting through this heavenly council, the celestial band of envoys and viceroys, servants and messengers who perform his will.

Transcendence and Immanence

What the Jew is wrestling with in this language of a heavenly council is one of the most profound and difficult of all theological-philosophical problems: the problem of *transcendence* and *immanence*. Transcendence talks about the otherness of God, the fact that God is different from man, different from the world, independent, not confined to this world, majestic in his own right. Philosophers have always tried to insist that God exists in and of himself, completely independent of this world. That is what transcendence is trying to say. But notice this: you can make God so transcendent that he is completely severed from this world. We can so stress the otherness of God that we end up denying any real or living or continuing relationship of God to this world. That was the sad end result of the religious-philosophical movement called transcendentalism or deism. Early in the history of the infant thirteen colonies of the United States the deistic movement flourished. It stressed the otherness or the transcendentalism of God so completely that God ended up having nothing to do with the world. The world was seen as if it were a watch or a clock. In this view God wound it up and after that it ran all by itself. God was no longer involved. He was transcendent.

The other word, immanence, tries to avoid the

error of separating God from the world. Immanence stresses the fact that God *is* involved in this world, here and now, working within it. But immanence goes to the opposite extreme. It locks God up in this world, confines him to his creation, limits him to this world, and denies him any independent existence. That is called, philosophically, *pantheism*—the belief that this world is the whole show, and God is part of it.

That has always been the struggle of religion and philosophy! How to avoid those two extremes? How to understand God as independent or transcendent without separating him from the world? Or how to make him immanent, involved in the world, without limiting him only to this world? Abstract philosophical thought seems incapable of avoiding the extremes, incapable of holding these two opposite thoughts together in tension. But the Jew does not think abstractly or philosophically. He thinks concretely! And in this concrete word picture of a heavenly council headed by God, the Jew has held these two diverse ideas together in delicate beautiful tension. God is transcendent. He is not locked up in this world. He is on the other side of the heavenly council. He is surrounded by angels, seraphim, and cherubim. He is the transcendent ruler of all things, standing independently of the world. And yet he is also immanent, involved in the affairs of the world, ruling the lives of man—ruling not directly but indirectly through his heavenly council.

Angels

God, then, rules the world, indirectly, through his heavenly council. A further part of Jewish thought is the conviction that there is a specific group of angels in that heavenly council whose particular task is to display the love of God. These are servants whose function is to pour out on men the blessings and protection of the Lord God Most High. Here is the doctrine of guardian angels, angels whose one function is to look after the children of God. This doctrine finds expression on the lips of Jesus himself, so deeply rooted was it in Jewish thought. In Matthew 18:10 Jesus warns against abusing little children, insisting that those who do abuse such will have to account to God himself because God has special angels looking after those children: "See that you do not despise one of these little ones; for I tell you that in heaven their angels always behold the face of my Father who is in heaven." The same kind of worldview lies behind the passage in Acts 12. The apostle Peter is in prison. The church prays for his release, imploring God to liberate their leader. And God does. But not directly. Indirectly. He sends an angel. A guardian angel, one of the heavenly host. Acts 12:7, ". . . and behold, an angel of the Lord appeared . . ." and then follows Peter's release.

Counterpoised to this group of angels whose task it was to express the love or protection of God, there was another group whose task it was to express the wrath or displeasure of God. These were the ones charged with raining disaster on the face of the earth, causing woe and havoc. For example, in the story of the ten plagues in Egypt in the Exodus narrative, Pharaoh was repeatedly urged and warned to let the people go. When he refused, the tenth and climactic plague was the death of the firstborn of every Egyptian household. For failure to obey, the punishment was death. Decreed by God, Pharaoh was about to be punished. At that critical moment, after reading all along that it was *God's* will that the punishment fall, we then read that when the punishment does fall, it is not God who delivers it but rather his servant, the destroyer, the angel of death. Read carefully Exodus 12:23 and you will see that the will of God is being worked, but it is worked indirectly, through his servant the destroyer.

Now notice that these angel servants of wrath are charged with an unhappy function. Theirs is the unpleasant task of causing terror and suffering on the face of the earth. From the viewpoint of their work, they are not very pleasant to have around. But nonetheless they are loyal servants of the living God. Though they are charged with death and punishment, wrath and woe, *never* are we allowed to see them as enemies of God working in opposition to his holy will. On the contrary, they are charged with executing his will and carrying out his righteous judgments. A modern example would be the executioner in a prison. His is not a happy task. He brings an end to life. He causes suffering both on the individual and on the family of the doomed person. But even though in one sense his work is destructive, that in no way alters the fact that he is a loyal servant of the state, is paid a salary every month, and works within the approved framework of justice. He is a servant, not an enemy.

Satan the Servant

And it is precisely in that sense that Satan is seen in the Old Testament, not as an enemy but as a servant. Do you know what the word "Satan" literally means? It is not a name, like Ralph, or Michael, John, or Gabriel. It is instead a title. It has a meaning. The word "Satan" in Hebrew means, literally, "the adversary." And everyone who has ever seen a Perry Mason television courtroom scene knows that the word "adversary" is a legal term. Our whole American judicial or legal system is built on what we call the adversary system. When you go into court there are two lawyers present. One is on your side, the counsel for the defense, the defense attorney. He is your advocate, the one who takes your side. (Indeed, in French, the word for lawyer is *avocat*, advocate, the one who takes your side.) But on the other side, there is the adversary, the one who brings in the indictment and tries to prove you guilty. He is the public prosecutor, the district attorney, the servant of the state bringing in charges and trying to prove those charges. That is what the word "Satan" means in the Old Testament—the adversary, the prosecuting attorney, the district attorney, the legal arm of the heavenly council. Satan is the servant of God whose specific task is to seek out the guilty and try them.

With that as background we are ready to turn to the only passage in the entire Old Testament that speaks of Satan at length—Job chapter one.

As we read that chapter we see that the heavenly council has been called to a meeting. All the angel-servants of God have been summoned to give their reports. And right there in the midst of the loyal sons or servants of God stands Satan. Job 1:6, "Now there was a day when the sons of God came to present themselves before the Lord, and Satan also came among them." We say to ourselves, because of our New Testament perspective, "What is Satan, the enemy of God, doing there in fellowship with the faithful?" But that is the point. In the Old Testament he is not an enemy, but a servant—the district attorney, responsible for spying out the lawless and sinful.

Then Satan is summoned to make his report. God asks where he has been, what he has been doing.

And Satan responds, "From going to and fro on the earth, and from walking up and down on it." One hesitates to use modern language for fear of sounding cute or coy—but you have to take that chance. What the answer means, in modern terminology, is that Satan, like any good law-enforcement officer has been walking his beat, looking for wrongdoers.

The conversation continues, "Have you considered my servant Job?" God asks. "There is none like him on the earth, a blameless and upright man, who fears God and turns away from evil" (Job 1:8).

Satan is asked to evaluate Job. And what is Satan's task as district attorney? To bring in indictments, to file charges. And that is what he does. He accuses Job of feigning piety, of pretending faith, of only going through the motions of true belief, of taking advantage of God to reap the benefits poured out by the guardian angels. "Does Job fear God for naught? Hast thou not put a hedge about him and his house and all that he has, on every side? Thou hast blessed the work of his hands, and his possessions have increased in the land. But put forth thy hand now, and touch all that he has, and he will curse thee to thy face" (Job 1:9-11). There is the indictment, the accusation.

Translate that into modern English, and what Satan is saying is something like this: "Sure, Job gives a good appearance. And why not? Every time he turns around his camel has another calf. You have made blessings bubble out of his ears. He has been taking advantage of you, God. He is not a true believer—he is only pretending faith to reap the benefits. He is really a baldfaced liar and a blackguard at heart, and you can see it for yourself if you take away his possessions. Then he will reveal his true colors—he will blaspheme to your very face. *That* is the kind of man he really is!"

The indictment has been lodged. The trial will now take place. Satan is allowed to bring Job to the test. "And the Lord said to Satan, 'Behold, all that he has is in your power; only upon himself do not put forth your hand'" (Job 1:12). Then Satan goes forth, and the roof falls in on Job.

But underline this in your thinking, or else you will never understand Old Testament thought. Satan does not go out to try Job until he gets God's permission, nor does he ever go further than the guidelines laid down by God, "only upon himself do not put forth your hand." Satan never goes off independently, nor does he go further than God's limits. He does not, because in the Old Testament he is considered a loyal servant, a member of the heavenly council, one of the sons of God.

That brings us back to where we started the chapter. The whole of the Old Testament doctrine of Satan can be summed up in two words—insignificant, and a servant. Mentioned only three times, only once at length, and in that one lengthy passage, a loyal servant. That is *all* that the Old Testament has to say about Satan! Any more than that is untrue to the Old Testament.

But when one opens the New Testament, what a dramatic reversal. In the New Testament Satan is no longer insignificant but central. And no longer a servant but an enemy. Indeed not "an" enemy but "the" enemy—the overarching malignant foe against whom the entire ministry of Jesus is aimed. One cannot read the New Testament intelligently unless one recognizes that the one central thrust of its pages is to affirm and ardently insist that Jesus has come to destroy the devil and all his works and all his ways.

Where is the change? The Old Testament presents Satan as an insignificant enemy. The New Testament says that he is the very embodiment of evil enmity towards God. Obviously, the change came between the Old and the New Testament and to that period we now turn.

II

Satan in the Intertestamental Period

The story of Satan in the Intertestamental period does not begin with Satan and it does not begin in the Intertestamental period. The roots are deeper, older than that. It all began about four centuries before Jesus was born. It began when a rugged young Greek warrior strapped on the sword, and at the age when most men are learning how to shave, conquered the world. His armies rolled out of northern Greece, rolled across the Hellespont from Europe into Asia, smashed the Persian fleet at Issus in 333 B.C., and swung the pendulum of power from east to west where it remained for the next 2000 years. The battles this young warrior won were of such heroic stature that the world ever since has superfluously added "the Great" to his name, Alexander.

Alexander the Great

The strength of Alexander was that he was a magnificent soldier. His men revered him like one of the gods. Convinced that he was indestructible they took incredible chances, and dared the odds and the elements. His soldiers were electrified by his magnetic leadership. The story is told that one day the armies of Alexander were pursuing the Persian soldiers across the Anatolian plains of modern-day Turkey when they were unexpectedly halted by a raging stream, swollen by the melting snows flowing down from the Anatolian hills. Alexander came up, pushed his horse in, armor and all, miraculously made it to the other side, and his men, so inspired by his example, went in as well, made it to the other side, and fell on the sleeping Persians a few miles farther on—sleeping, because they were convinced no mere man could make it across the swollen stream. But Alexander was no mere man. His men adored him.

Another time, Alexander wanted ships to move into the Orient. Where to get them? From Tyre, the island city lying off the coast of modern-day Lebanon. But how capture an island city without ships? And it was precisely because he had no ships that he wanted to capture Tyre! The solution? Alexander set aside 10,000 troops who did nothing but carry rocks, filling in the land, building a causeway from shore to the island, and when it was completed he took the city, captured the ships, and sailed toward the Orient! Aggressive audacity, tempestuous confidence, daring imagination, Alexander was a great soldier, it was his strength.

But in the economy of life a virtue is often a vice, a strength a weakness. The very things that make us strong may render us weak. Where, for example, do tenacity and perseverance (a virtue) shade off into stubbornness (a vice)? Strengths are weaknesses. The strength of Alexander was that he was a great soldier. But that very strength, that very concentration on his military prowess, turns out to be a weakness in the long sweep of history, for it camouflages the true greatness of Alexander. He was not basically a soldier: he was an evangelist! He was driven to the ends of the earth by a dream, a vision, a lofty goal.

No man conquers for lust alone. It is not negative raw ambition that leads one to breast the tide of worldly fortune. To do the things Alexander did, one must be propelled by loftier motives than power alone. Alexander had a dream, a vision. He was an evangelist—an evangelist for man. Locked up in Alexander's brain was an extraordinary concept of man as a giant, master of his fate, controller of his own destiny—and that dream Alexander wanted to share. He wanted to announce the good news of man's independence and potential, that man was the master of his own fate, the captain of his own ship.

From where that dream? Behind every great man there is a great . . . what? Don't answer "woman." Enough of that female chauvinism! Behind every great man there is a great *teacher*. And Alexander had a great teacher, the famous Aristotle. It was from Aristotle that the young Alexander soaked in the soaring ideal of man as a giant. The story is told—perhaps untrue but nonetheless it sums up the essence of the influence of Aristotle on his pupil—that one day the aged teacher and the young lad were sitting in a cave in northern Greece as the young Alexander was doing his homework. Aristotle, patient, musing, was poking at a small fire, boiling a pot of water, brewing a cup of tea. And as he poked and mused, he suddenly leaped to his feet, transfixed by what he had seen, and shouted out, "Alexander, I have found it!"

"What?" was the obvious answer. "The secret of rainfall!" The kettle, hit by the flames of the fire below, had been giving off steam. Water vapor was drifting upward in the cave, and when that rising steam hit the cool rocks of the cave overhead it condensed to droplets of water. "I have found it, Alexander, the secret of rainfall. It is like that in the broad world of nature. The sun is the fire. It makes the water vapor rise up off the streams and pools, the sea and the lakes, and when that water vapor rises to the cool heavens above, it condenses and falls as drops of rain. Alexander, do you realize what this means? It means that man can make rain. It may take awhile to figure out how to build fires that large —but that is only a technical problem. We know the secret. Man no longer has to live hemmed in by narrow river valleys, no longer has to farm on the fertile plains alone, but now we can make the deserts bloom. We can transform the face of the earth into a garden."

That was the dream that Alexander got from his teacher—the vision of man as a giant, with the secrets of the universe locked up in his brain. With thought, with intensive research and aggressive ingenuity, man could unfold the mysteries of nature, control the cosmos, transform the world, mold and master his own destiny. That was the dream of Alexander, the good news of man, that he wanted to share with the whole world. And that is why, when the armies of Alexander rolled, they had not only the soldier's sword but the librarian's card as well. The city he founded in north Africa, Alexandria, had the world's largest library!

Alexander conquered the world at 21. At 33 he was dead. But his dream of the might of man never died. When he died, his world empire was divided into quadrants, and each of the four parts eventually became independent empires ruled by one of his generals. These Greek generals became kings, and gave rise to dynasties, sons who ruled as kings after them. The general-king who concerns us is the one who had his seat of power in modern-day Syria, just north of the Holy Land, the home of the Jews. This king eventually took the name of Antiochus, and was followed by Antiochus II, Antiochus III, and Antiochus IV. When we get to Antiochus IV the year is now about 180 B.C., the Intertestamental period.

Antiochus Epiphanes—Persecution

Antiochus IV did not want to be merely a number, so he threw away the "IV" and took for himself the descriptive title "Epiphanes." Antiochus Epiphanes was destined to be the grimmest, foulest name in all history until the time of Adolph Hitler. The very name is revelatory. "Epiphanes" comes from two Greek words, *epi* and *phanos*. *Phanos* means torch or lantern, and *epi* means on, upon . . . "The shining lantern." What Antiochus was calling himself was the light of the world. What light would he shed? He would revitalize the ancient ideal of Alexander, the gigantic proportions and powers of man. He would preach anew the gospel of Alexander, that man was a giant and the master of his own fate. And to whom would he preach it? Why, obviously, to the peoples under his sway . . . to the Jews living just south of Syria.

And the Jews, hearing of the good news of mighty man, firmly rejected the message. Theirs was a heritage that magnified not man but God! "The earth is the *Lord's* and the fulness thereof" sang the psalmist. "In the beginning, *God*. . . ." Moses had told them. It was God, not man, who cradled the seas and shaped the majestic mountains. It was God, not mere man, who was the source of life, and the architect of the universe. And the Jew rejected the man-centered human-exalting philosophy of Antiochus Epiphanes.

Epiphanes was infuriated. Infuriated but not stopped. He recognized that before he could plant Greek philosophy he had to rip up Jewish theology; before one can plant one must plow. And plow and rip he did indeed! He unleashed the most devastating persecution the Jews had ever known. The Jew had known trouble before. He was born in the iron furnace of Egypt, he had seen his ten northern tribes savagely decimated by the atrocities of Assyria, Nebuchadnezzar of Babylon had burned out the eyes of King Zedekiah, leveled the walls of Jerusalem, shattered the temple, the Persians had executed Zerubbabel and held the nation as hostage. All this the Jews had known before. But never before had they suffered a vicious attack like the one Antiochus unleashed, for Antiochus was ripping at their very soul, trying to destroy the spiritual spinal column of the nation. He was attacking their religion, the rock on which they stood.

The first thing he did was proscribe the reading of the Law. If anyone was found reading the Books of Moses, death! He fouled and defiled the temple. All Jews, ancient and modern look upon pork as unclean, the pig as defiling. And Antiochus ran a whole herd of pigs into the temple, and there he had them butchered, their blood oozing over the temple altar, desecrating the sanctuary. (Eventually, under the Maccabees, the Jews won that temple back, purified it, reconsecrated it to God, and lit the candles anew. That feast of lights, commemorating the cleansing of the temple, is still practiced to this very day—Hanukkah. In Hanukkah, the vivid and vicious memory of the infamy of Antiochus Epiphanes lives on,

the blackest, grimmest name in all of Jewish history
. . . until Auschwitz, Bergen-Belsen, and Dachau,
under Adolph Hitler, gave them an even grimmer
enemy.)

But even this was only the beginning of the agony
heaped on the Jews by Epiphanes. Every Jewish lad
was to be circumcized on the eighth day of his life.
Epiphanes decreed that any baby so circumcized was
to be put to death. The priest who performed the
sacrament was to be slain. The father of the dead
child was to be executed immediately, and the dead
body of the murdered child was to be fastened
around the neck of the mother.

Out of this night of terror came an agonizing reappraisal of all that the Jew believed. There came
a convulsive reshaping of Jewish society that formed
the very framework of the society in which Jesus
lived. Every Jewish sect and party that parades
across the pages of the New Testament was born
in this hour of horror.

Pharisees and Sadducees

How did the Jews react? How would any people
react? Some ran, some fought, some surrendered
and went to the other side. There were those who
took the easy way out by going to Antiochus' way of
thinking. They adopted Greek philosophy, and became "Greek" Jews. This is the party that survives
in the New Testament as the Sadducees. The Sadducees were the ones who abandoned the essence
of Jewish thought and took up Greek ways.

One can see evidence of this in the New Testament itself. In Acts 23:6-8 the apostle Paul is on
trial before the Jews, fighting for his life. When he
notices that his jury is part Sadducee and part

Pharisee he cries out that he is on trial because he believes in the reality of the resurrection, and with that he splits the jury and remains unconvicted. He could do that because he knew that the Sadducees had adopted Greek thought, whereas the Pharisees had stayed true to Jewish thought.

Greek thought believed that man was divided into two parts, body and spirit, and, further, that only the spirit was eternal, only the spirit survived death. The Greek, and the Sadducee after him, believed not in the resurrection of the body but in the immortality of the soul, that only the soul survived. But the Hebrew believed that God had made the whole man, body as well as spirit or soul, so the Jew —the Pharisee—believed in the resurrection of the body, and Paul thus split the jury: ". . . 'with respect to the hope and the resurrection of the dead I am on trial.' And when he had said this, a dissension arose between the Pharisees and the Sadducees; and the assembly was divided. For the Sadducees say that there is no resurrection, nor angel, nor spirit; but the Pharisees acknowledge them all."

Because the Sadducees were willing to adopt the ways of the oppressor, the oppressor catapulted them to power, used them, pushed them forward and gave them authority, made them priests and rulers over the people, hoping thus to control the population through them. In this way the most corrupt element in Jewish society, the compromising Sadducees, became the priests. No wonder that Jesus never has a kind word or a civil conversation with the Sadducees. Instead he drives their lackeys from the temple with a whip.

But some fought. Some strove to retain their Jewish heritage regardless of cost. And those were the Pharisees, the noblest element of the Jewish population. If one can rightly call the Sadducees the "Greek" Jews the only proper name for the Pharisees is the "Jewish" Jews. True, by the time one moves from the days of Epiphanes to the time of Jesus some of the Pharisees have degenerated into smug and pious holier-than-thou hypocrites, and that is what Jesus labels them. But their eventual descent into smug self-righteousness should never be allowed to discolor or camouflage the heroic stand they took in the face of adversity. In that grim and dangerous hour when their lives were at stake, the Pharisees fought for the purity of the Jewish religion, no matter what the cost.

The Essenes

Yet another sect was born during this troubled time. Not only the Sadducees and the Pharisees find their historical origins in this period, but a third party also came into being, a third party that neither compromised, nor fought, but fled. They are given little literary notice in the New Testament, but in recent years the discovery of the Dead Sea Scrolls has enabled us to see the full dimensions of their convictions. These were the Essenes, the group that went to live in places like Qumran on the shores of the Dead Sea.

The Dead Sea basin is the most hostile, barren, sterile, forsaken place on the face of the earth. By 10 o'clock in the morning, the temperature is already 110°. Nothing grows in this stark, arid, bitter, and deserted land, the lowest place on the face of the earth. The entire basin has only one place that is fertile and green, the northeastern corner, where the fresh waters of the Jordan finish their long run down from Syria and empty into and die in the Dead Sea.

There in the Jordan valley is life and greenery. Here Jericho, a beautiful oasis, is located. Near Jericho. Moses once sent in the spies who saw the fertility of this place and came back and reported that it was "a land of milk and honey" yielding grapes as large as watermelons. Jericho is the only fertile place in the Dead Sea basin.

And yet the Essenes lived on the opposite side of the Dead Sea, the barren west, cramped in below the foreboding Judean hills that reflected the searing sun, intensifying the heat, burning skin and plant alike. Why there? Why did the Essenes pick not only the worst place on the face of the earth to live, but even the worst part of that worst place? Because they were convinced that the very earth had gone amuck, had slipped away from the sovereignty of God, had fallen prey to the devil. That is why they abandoned the world and all its pleasures. They believed the world and its ways were not under God's rule but under the sway of Satan. That is why the Essenes fled the world. Why would anyone embrace what belonged to the evil one? That is why the Essenes gave up on private property, renounced marriage, ate so little, humiliated the body by exposing it and wearing only a loin cloth.

We know from excavations at Qumran that there was no such thing as private property. All things were held communally. All meals were shared (all the plates were found in one room in the excavations). If a husband and a wife joined the community, they parted from one another never to see each other again. Why would a person want to procreate and bring forth sons and daughters to live in Satan's realm? The theology of the Essenes—their conviction that the world was under the rule of

Satan in the Intertestamental Period 37

Satan—accounts for the place and the way they lived.

If one stopped with that description of the Essenes they would sound negative indeed, world-renouncing, pessimistic, convinced of the supremacy of Satan. But we cannot stop there. We cannot know the Essenes until and unless we recognize that they were basically optimistic. Yes, indeed, the world was under the power of the devil—the atrocities afflicted on the people by Antiochus Epiphanes proved that. But God would act again and destroy the devil and all his works and all his ways. One of the most famous of all the Dead Sea Scrolls left to us by the Essenes is entitled "The War of the Sons of Light and the Sons of Darkness." This scroll insists that the world is under the evil legions of Satan, the sons of darkness, but God will have the last word. The sons of God, the angels of light, will come and destroy the evil foe, smash the rule of Satan, and restore the kingdom of God. In the despair under Antiochus was born the hope of renewal, the confident conviction that God would act again with great power.

We have gone into this lengthy discussion of the views of the Essenes because those views hold the key to the solution of the question we asked at the end of the previous chapter: when and how did Satan undergo the transformation from the Old Testament view of him as an insignificant servant to the New Testament view of him as an overarching enemy? It happened in the persecutions of Antiochus Epiphanes. Those catastrophic calamities of Antiochus not only reshaped Jewish society and produced the Sadducees, the Pharisees, and the Essenes. They produced a whole new understanding of the nature and role of Satan.

The Principle of Retribution

Faced by the overwhelmingly brutal atrocities of Epiphanes, seeing on every side the miscarriage of justice, Jewish theological thought was shaken to its very roots. Earlier it was believed that God ruled the world and that he ruled it fairly and justly. The principle of retribution not only prevailed but dominated the Old Testament. The principle of retribution is but a fancy theological way of saying "an eye for an eye and a tooth for a tooth."

Our problem with that principle is twofold. One, we usually see it only in negative terms. That is, we think of it only in terms of revenge. If one hurts me, puts out my eye, I have the right (even the obligation, to satisfy justice) of putting out his eye. But the principle was not merely negative, allowing revenge. It was also positive, demanding reward. If someone hurt me, I could give retribution. But if someone aided me, I was to help others. Not only evil for evil, but good for good.

The second problem we usually have with that principle is that ordinarily we see only its horizontal dimension, how it governs man-to-man relationships. If my neighbor hurts me, or helps me, I am to hurt, or to help him. But in Jewish thought it was not merely horizontal, governing man-to-man relationships. It was also vertical, governing the God-man relationship. If I was good in the eyes of God, he would reward me. If I sinned in the eyes of God, he would punish me. When I did right in God's eyes, he would send one of his angels of love to minister to me, look after me, guard over me. But if I disobeyed his will, one of the avenging members of the heavenly council would swoop in on me and bring judgment on my head.

This is what we mean when we say that the Old Testament contains a religion of law, a religion of merit. Man gets what he has coming to him. His piety will affect his destiny. The good will be prospered by God and the evil will be punished. Psalm 1 is an example of this point of view. Read that psalm. Notice how its six verses are divided symetrically into two distinct halves. The first three verses deal with the good man, the one who walks not in the ways of the wicked, and those first three verses end with the insistence that the good man "in all that he does he shall prosper." The principle of retribution, vertically understood, says that God will reward the good man. But the next three verses deal with the opposite side of the coin, concentrating on the evil man. The psalm closes with the insistence at the end of verse six that "the way of the wicked shall perish."

The Old Testament emphasizes the conviction that God is master of the whole world, that he rules through his heavenly council, rewarding the good and punishing the evil. One could measure a man's piety by looking at his wealth. If one suffered, it was because he was sinful. But the Old Testament also wrestles with exceptions to that principle. The Book of Job is a profound struggle with the inexplicable mystery of why in Job's case the principle was not true. Job was a good man, yet he suffered. Why? The problem is wrestled with, but never answered. The final "solution" of the Book of Job is to counsel us to patience, that in the mysteries of God there is a solution, but it is not known to us.

That kind of answer (if it is an answer) provided in Job—namely, be patient—was alright earlier when there was only an occasional case of apparent injustice, only an isolated case of an innocent or good man suffering. But in the holocaust of Antiochus Epiphanes it was no longer an occasional or isolated exception. The whole society had gone berserk! The very opposite of justice prevailed. The wicked, corrupt, and compromising Sadducee was catapulted ahead. And it was the Pharisee who fought for freedom of religion. It was the loyal servant of God who suffered. It was the devout mother who took her child to the temple to have him circumcized, who tried to fulfill the expressed will of God. It was she who saw her child butchered like an animal and his carcass draped around her neck. All hell seemed to have broken loose. There was no justice in the world. The very opposite of the principle of retribution was in operation. The evil prospered and the good were ground down, their teeth broken, their lives destroyed! Where was the God of justice?

In that horrendous hour the Jew agonizingly appraised his whole concept of how God governed the world. Earlier it was believed that Satan was a servant executing the will of God, punishing the evil on God's behalf. But now, in the face of rampant suffering and vicious violations of fair play, the Jew came to the conviction that something had happened upstairs. Satan had revolted. A war had taken place in heaven. The former servant had become rebellious and had led his wing of the heavenly council in insurrection against God.

Satan—From Servant to Enemy

Jewish literature of this period, commonly called apocalyptic literature, is dominated by the accounts of the revolt of the heavenly council and the fall of Satan, his metamorphosis from servant to enemy. The Book of Enoch has two separate accounts of the fall of the angels. The Book of Jubilees has its own account. Other books could be mentioned. But all of these could be dismissed, set aside as Jewish fantasy, except for one fact of Scripture.

These non-canonical Jewish books of apocalyptic literature are not the only ones that insist on the fall of Satan. That idea is engrained in the very substance of the New Testament also. In Revelation 12:7ff. we read these words: "Now war arose in heaven, Michael and his angels fighting against the dragon; and the dragon and his angels fought, but they were defeated and there was no longer any place for them in heaven. And the great dragon was thrown down, that ancient serpent, who is called the Devil and Satan, the deceiver of the whole world—he was thrown down to the earth, and his angels were thrown down with him." The revolt was quelled upstairs. All was put in order up there and peace was restored. Thus the passage can continue in verse 12: "Rejoice then, O heaven and you that dwell therein!" Certainly they can rejoice up there, for the violent interloper has been expelled. But where did he go? To the earth. And so the sentence just quoted continues, "But woe to you, O earth and sea, for the devil has come down to you in great wrath, for he knows that his time is short."

That was the way the Jew accounted for the atrocities of Antiochus Epiphanes. He insisted that the frightful perversions of fairplay were not the will of God but the work of the enemy of God, Satan, working through his agent of evil, Antiochus Epiphanes. Notice well, the Jewish discussion of the fall of the angels is not mere abstract philosophy, not merely idle speculation on the nature of the celestial scene above. He was wrestling with a problem, a deadly problem, the awesome extent of tragedy in the immediate world—and that tragedy he traced back not to God but to Satan.

Before we go any further, we must pause to look clearly at what the doctrine of Satan, his revolt against God and his emergence as the archenemy of all goodness, is trying to say—and also what it is *not* saying, which in one sense is even more important.

One thing not often enough noticed about the biblical doctrine of Satan is that it is philosophically naive. It truly is an inadequate and unsatisfactory doctrine when analyzed rationally and logically. It leaves so many answers ungiven, so many issues unresolved. The Sadducees, the heirs of Greek philosophical thought, eventually saw the philosophical-rational weakness of the doctrine of Satan and that is why they rejected it. Notice well that in the passage we quoted earlier, Acts 23:8, the Sadducees reject the belief in the resurrection. They also reject any belief in spirits as well. The doctrine of Satan is intellectually unsatisfactory. Why? Because, as said, there are so many things it does *not* say.

For example, we today, with our modern philosophical and rational approach to reality, pose all kinds of questions about Satan. Why did he fall? When did he fall? Why did God create him? Why does God tolerate his continued existence? And on and on the list of questions can go. And the significant thing is that the Jew wrestled with not one of those issues. Take for example the question of when Satan fell. When did the war in heaven take place? One school of Jewish thinking argued that Satan must have fallen right then, in the time of Antiochus, about the year 180 B.C., for it was in that moment that the red scar of arbitrary caprice began to rip through men's lives making mockery of their aspirations and crushing their ideals. But another school of

Jewish scholars argued that the satanic fall must have taken place much earlier, for after all, was there not always trouble in the world? Had not even Adam and Eve been tempted in the garden at the very beginning? And this school therefore concluded that the fall of Satan had taken place even before the world began. It was this school of thought, then, that went on to identify the serpent in the garden with Satan, the deceiver of the world.

Neither of these schools of thought ever prevailed, one vanquishing the other. They were allowed to stand side by side, unresolved. And *that* is what is significant. Obviously, if the Jew never finally got around to making up his mind as to precisely when Satan fell, then the exact time of Satan's fall was not an important issue. And the same thing can be said about all the other philosophical-rational questions we raise. Why did he fall? Why did God create him? These are not the essential issues. The doctrine of Satan does not even treat those issues. That is not what is important. The doctrine of Satan is not speaking to that. What, then, *is* the important issue?

The Will of God

The very heart of the doctrine of Satan is not so much a statement about Satan as much as it is a statement about God. The one thing that the Jew is seeking to assert in his insistence on the fall of Satan is *that God is not the author of tragedy!* The vicious destruction of human life, the searing battering of human destiny, is not the will of God. It is the work of God's enemy. The doctrine of Satan is really saying two things, related and yet separate.

On the one hand, the doctrine of Satan is an affirmation of faith in the purity and holiness of God. By ascribing all suffering to God's enemy, what the Jew is really saying is that he does not believe in a God who maims and cripples. He does not believe in an arbitrary capricious God who wantonly persecutes. These things are incompatible with the will of God. God is not evil. He does not cause unfair pain or undue suffering. Wherever and however suffering gets started, one thing is sure: it is not in God. It is in the enemy of God that such violence finds its bitter seed.

The other thing which the doctrine of Satan is thundering is its adamant insistence on the fact that there *are* things that transpire in this world which are fundamentally opposed to the idea of a just and ruling God. It is only later misguided Christian piety that tries to trace all things back to the will of God. Cancer strikes a loved one, and we bow our head and say "the will of God." Hurricanes rip the Carribbean, earthquakes rock Alaska, typhoons capsize boats in the Pacific, crop failures cause millions to starve, wars rip and ravage entire populations, and we bow our heads and say "the will of God." Not the Jew! He looked at the immense and awesome tragedy running roughshod over suffering people and he refused to trace it back to God. He insisted on the reality of evil forces active in the world in direct opposition to God. He courageously faced the fact of want and deprivation. He realistically observed that not all that happens in this world can be called "good" or traced back to God.

To his credit, the Jew of yesteryear did not paint over human suffering and call it the will of God. He realistically and ardently and eloquently insisted that we live in a strange and alien world where all of our hopes can be smashed by caprice. We live in a fallen cosmos where anguish and pain are constant companions. The Jew called facts by their right names. He did not camouflage pain by calling it a blessing. He asserted what we all recognize in the pit of our stomach and in the dark frames of our haunted imagination, that there are devilish powers afoot. He saw that there was evil in the world, evil that loomed even larger than God.

Seeds of Despair

Our modern society has been dragged, struggling all the way, to the same conclusion. The optimistic enthusiasm of an earlier age has been washed away by the flood of a rising pessimism, an evergrowing tension of despair lurking below the very surface of our society. We, too, in our time have had to face the fact of awesome evil making mockery of all our hopes. We have been ravaged by two World Wars in one generation, sandwiched around a depression, followed in turn by a third World War that no one bothered to number, the Korean conflict. But those tragedies of the past have been transcended by the shock of Vietnam, the most costly war in all of American history. The divisive convulsive struggle of Vietnam left cruel marks greater than anything the nation had ever known before. More men were lost, maimed, wounded in those wars of Vietnam than in any other struggle in our nation's life. And the tragedy of it is that it still goes on! We may talk about "peace with honor," but the simple irrefutable fact is that they never did have the fife and bugle corps play "When Johnny Comes Marching Home Again" after Vietnam, for it never ended! We may have brought our American troops home, but the struggle continues.

That is the fuel of despair. And the movement toward despair is accelerated by other events of recent years. Vietnam was but one side of the darkening cloud hanging over a near-despairing people. While some young men were losing their lives in the senseless war of a faraway land, youth at home were engaged in their own war. Our campuses across the land were aflame with dissidents, with radicals, with pugnacious, brawling, bombing students. In the late 60s Stanford University, one of the finest academic institutions in the land, was in moral decay. The University of California at Berkeley—a magnificent school with more Nobel prize winners on its faculty than any other university in the world—was a moral cesspool. On the University of Wisconsin campus a bomb exploded in one of its laboratories. Innocent people were killed. The ivory tower had become a frontline fortress. The university that was to be training the finest qualities of young minds, raising them up for significant contributions to unending progress, were boiling centers of riot. In more recent times the word Watergate brings a sense of shame and discouragement to everyone who loves his land. This is the fuel on the fire of our discontent, the substructure of the near panic of our time, that has torn away our delusion of the grandeur of man and has brought us perilously close to despair.

Vietnam, Watergate. Why limit ourselves to these momentous issues of national and international affairs? A while back I could not even buy $3.00 worth of gasoline for my car. The energy shortage was ravaging our nation. Not even $3.00 worth of gas. It is insulting. What has happened to the marvelous America we hymn in our Thanksgiving songs, that land spilling its bounty and largess from sea to shining sea?

I remember the tender, touching moment I had

with my father the summer before I started college. We were sitting out on the front stoop in the city of Chicago during August of 1946, perspiring. That is what one did for recreation in Chicago in August —perspire. I looked at that old Greek immigrant, now turning gray, being burned out by a menial job in one of the many factories of sprawling Chicago, wearing out his life's blood pulling on the handle of a punch press to save up enough money to send his oldest son to *college*. And I was going to go—and answer the dream of an immigrant born across the waters in a land shorn of all hope, where poverty was perennial and the castes closed.

He told me of his dream. He spoke of the vision that had lured him across the Atlantic to the brave new world. In broken English, unpolished by the niceties of education, he told me about that lady who stood out in the harbor of New York with the water splashing round her feet, the one who had those words written at the base, "Give me your tired, your poor." In response to that dream he left family and friends behind and joined the stream of immigrants coming from the Peloponnesian Peninsula in Greece, from the flinty hills of Norway, from the Black Forest of Germany, coming to a new land where even a punch press operator could send his son to *college*. The dream. And then the day came when I could not even buy $3.00 worth of gas. Insulting!

This is the temper of our times. We are thrown by the irony of history into the same steaming cauldron as the Jew of yesteryear. The powers of evil are evident and in the ascendancy. There is no stability, nothing on which one can lean anymore. The old familiar landmarks are gone. The peace of an earlier day has evaporated. The horsemen of war, pestilence, and plague are joined by the betrayers of public trust. There is a frightening parallel between the collapse of our confidence and the shattered convictions of the Jew. They then saw the reality of Satan for the first time. And that is true of us as well.

For the first time in American history the doctrine of Satan has moved to the fore. We, like the Jews of old, are overwhelmed by the shocking realization that there are inexplicable forces of evil active in our cosmos. We have seen the explosion in our time of a belief in the demonic. There is despair afoot, and indeed, despair is the only possible eventuality if one stops at that point. If one merely recognizes the reality of evil and then says no more, all that there can be is despair. That is the condemnation of modern talk about the devil—it stops right there.

But the Jew did not stop on a note of despair. The biblical doctrine of Satan does not stop by insisting that suffering is real and Satan is an enemy of God. That is but the beginning of the doctrine of Satan, not the conclusion. The conclusion to the doctrine of Satan is found not in the Intertestamental period, but in the New Testament. To that we now turn.

III

Satan in the New Testament

The New Testament picks up where apocalyptic thought, where Essene thought, leaves off. The New Testament accepts the awesome reality of the devil and emphasizes his pervasive power. This is seen in the very circumstances of the beginning of Jesus' ministry. He is baptized by John the Baptist, probably an Essene. John is baptizing less than two miles from Khirbit Qumran, the home base of the Essenes. Everything we know about John identifies him with that group. They wore practically no clothing as a sign of self-abasement. John wore a camel-skin loincloth. They ate almost no food, disdaining the body because it was exposed to the influence of the evil one. John ate locusts. Essenes were celibate, giving up sex and marriage in order not to bring more children into a world ruled by the evil one. John was alone in the wilds of Judea. They were convinced, however, that God would triumph and restore his rule over a cosmos captured by the evil one. They affirmed that the angels of God, the sons of light, would triumph over the forces of Satan, the sons of darkness. And John's first words were that the kingdom of God, the restoration of God's rule, was at hand. To this man, trained in Essene thought and theology, Jesus comes to be baptized.

The Baptism of John

A word must be said about John's view of baptism, what it accomplished, what its purpose was. Its purpose grows right out of Essene beliefs in the power of the evil one. The entire world was estranged by God, seized by Satan, writhing in bondage. But such was not to endure forever. God was on the move! He was about to destroy the devil and all his works and all his ways. He was preparing to send the sons of light to destroy the sons of darkness, repeal their rule, and re-establish his own sovereignty.

But Satan would not surrender without fighting back. As the rule of God approached, the wrath of Satan would mount. Cosmic war was imminent. A time of destruction, woe, and trial unparalleled in human history was about to explode. There had been wars and rumors of wars in the past, but always in the past the antagonists were humans fighting one another. This final battle, however, would transcend the limited efforts of feeble man. That final battle was to be a battle between overarching angel powers, and thus its scope and dimension would be without parallel, and man, lowly man, would be caught in the middle!

Who could stand in such an hour? How could lowly man expect to survive the final ordeal? He was powerless to resist the awesome advances of such an exalted foe as the devil. Unless God intervened—unless the Holy One threw over him a mantle of protection warding off the darts of Satan he could not survive. This is the background, purpose, and meaning of John's baptism. Baptism was that divine act of merciful intervention of a loving God, designed to protect his elect from the persecutions of the evil one. As God's rule approached, Satan would resist. He would strike back at God, and strike at those who identified with God. The elect, the people of God, were in danger because they were immediately exposed to satanic tribulation. They would be Satan's targets. But God would protect them by casting a shield over them to protect them from the wrath which was to come. John's baptism was precisely that kind of protective coating of God.

No other party in Judaism—not the Pharisees, not the Sadducees—practiced baptism, for no other party took Satan as seriously as did John and the Essenes. Pharisees and Sadducees had no baptism of their own. That is why those two groups come to John to be baptized, rather than to practitioners of their own sects (Matt. 3:7). Lustrations, ceremonial washings with water were used by the Pharisees and Sadducees. But their washings did not have the same theological orientations as the baptism of John. For them, their washings were external signs of internal resolutions. The arrow was upward, the direction completely different. For them, the washing was a concrete symbol of man's personal resolution. They would wash off the physical dirt of their body as an outward sign that they were internally or spiritually seeking to be better, to cleanse their soiled souls. Their washings were an act of man, upward, man offering himself to God, seeking to do better.

That was not John's view. For him the arrow was not upward. It was not an act of man. The arrow was downward. It was an act of God. God himself was active in baptism. It was a sacrament, a divine act, not a personal resolve or a human deed. In the act of baptism God was protecting the person, immunizing him from Satan, shielding him from the counterattack of the devil. Because John saw his baptism in that light he was furious when those not really dedicated to God seek refuge in his baptism. He sees the corrupt Sadducees and the pompous Pharisees rushing to receive his baptism which would protect them from Satan's fury, and he indignantly cries out, "Who warned *you* to flee from the wrath to come?" (Matt. 3:7), and goes on to refuse them baptism! He will not give to them the protection of God, for they are not on the side of God.

And Jesus comes to John. He knows that Jesus is the divine redeemer, the one sent of the Father to bind the strong Satan. Jesus knows that as the divine invader sent to shatter Satan and restore the kingdom of God he will be the prime target of Satanic attack. He knows from the stories he heard from his mother that his birth was a miraculous act, a work of God, the first event in the final act of the cosmic drama. He was sent of God, he is God's Son as he himself affirmed in the story of his appearance in the temple at 12 years of age. It is through him that the evil one is to be repulsed. And, as the representative of God, he is the prime enemy of Satan, most exposed to his attacks—and thus he goes to be baptized by John at the Jordan, to receive the whole armor of God that he might be able to withstand during that dark and difficult final day of cosmic battle when the sons of darkness are to be routed.

The Power of Satan

But one need not speculate on the baptism of Jesus alone to see the demonological orientation of

New Testament thought. One need not read between the lines to understand the meaning of John's baptism. The New Testament is far too abundantly seeded with affirmations of Satan's reign for us to concentrate solely on these oblique or indirect affirmations of Satan's sovereignty on the present scene. The New Testament, often and ardently, directly and unambiguously insists that Satan is the ruler of the present world.

1 John 5:19 flatly affirms that "the whole world is in the power of the evil one." In 2 Corinthians 4:4 Paul decisively calls Satan the "god of this world." And, even more dramatically, in the extended passage beginning in Ephesians 6:10, Paul makes starkly clear his own convictions as to who is in charge of the present situation. He exhorts his people to prepare for the final hour. He warns them that their real enemy is not flesh and blood, human impulses, evil existential personal intentions. Instead, he says, the real enemy is Satan, and therefore, to stand, they must wear "the whole armor of God, that you may be able to stand against the wiles of the devil."

He then goes on to describe the frightening dimension of Satanic power, insisting that we have to stand against that cosmic foe, the principalities and powers (his word for the fallen angels) who are "the *world rulers* of this present darkness . . . the spiritual host of wickedness in the heavenly places." World rulers, *kosmokratores,* the malignant superpowers literally in charge of the affairs and functions of a fallen world. It is precisely because Paul is totally convinced that the present world is estranged from God and ruled by the fallen powers and principalities that he can go on to speak of the present world as the *"evil* age" (Gal. 1:4).

The New Testament does not simply affirm that

Satan is in control of the world in which we live. It goes on to insist that every ill and woe to which man is heir originates in Satan. Suffering, tragedy, and pain are not just punishments of an angry God. They are attacks, weapons, evil malignant actions of an evil malignant ruler, Satan.

Sickness comes from Satan. How far removed we are from New Testament thought when we ascribe illness to God. When a loved one is struck with cancer, when some disease ravages us or our family, if we think theologically at all, we cry out, "Why has God done this to me? What have I done to deserve this from the hand of God?" O ye of little faith! Read the New Testament carefully and engrave in the layers of your memory the words of Jesus himself. He looks at a crippled woman bent over nearly double with some kind of curvature of the spine. He looks at this body-debilitating malady, and he explicitly insists that this illness is not the work of God but the will of Satan. "And ought not this daughter of Abraham *whom Satan bound* for eighteen years, be loosed from this bond on the sabbath day?" (Luke 13:16). And Paul, faithful to the thought of Jesus, sees sickness in precisely the same light, as a work of the evil one. In 2 Corinthians 12:7, Paul speaks of his own painful illness that afflicted him all of his Christian life, and insists that it originates in the evil one—"a thorn was given me in the flesh, *a messenger of Satan,* to harass me...."

And not only sickness but hunger as well. *Hunger,* body-wasting starvation, this too is a work of the evil one. Ancient apocalyptic literature abounds with the conviction that the failure of food supplies, vermin in the fruit, crop failure, not enough to eat, were all a work of the devil. And that thought too pervades the New Testament. Where the devil is, there is

Satan in the New Testament

deprivation. Jesus is alone with the devil in the wilderness for forty days and the first temptation is to turn the stones into bread and eat. Wherever the devil is active hunger and famine follow. The apostle Paul, in Romans 8:35, is cataloging the weapons of the evil principalities and powers with which they try to separate us from the love of God. And there in a prime place, along side of tribulation and distress, peril and sword, is *famine*. Hunger is a work of the devil.

But the essential weapon, the basic powerful weapon of the evil one, is not sickness or hunger. If you are sick, you can always hope for a cure. If you are hungry, you can pray for a harvest. Those weapons might be overcome. The one final ultimate weapon of the evil one for which there is no cure, from which there is no reprieve, is *death*. When the cold, unfeeling fingers of the tomb reach out, there is no hope. Death is the shattering of all our aspirations, the end of all our optimism.

One of our basic problems of comprehending the fulness of the gospel today is that we have 2000 years of Christian tradition standing in the way, coloring and distorting the original vision of the New Testament people. We live on this side of Easter, 2000 years on this side of Easter. We no longer look at death from the perspective of those who saw it from the other side of Easter, from the black side of that final Friday. We see death from the Christian perspective, always examining it as a portal to heaven, to fellowship with the Father. Struggle for a moment to let your Christian comprehension of death as overcome seep away. Strive to see death as it once was seen, before Easter, as the final end of all human striving. Seek to stand at the graveside of a father burying his only son, dead before his life really began. Seek to comprehend the agonizing note of finality wrapped up in the shrouds of death as you consign to the ground, with no promise of a life after death, your only son. Do that, and you will understand why the people of 2000 years ago never cosmeticized the grave, never sought to perfume the fact of death, but saw it instead as an enemy. As a work of the devil. As the evil final triumph of Satan. When Satan acted in death he destroyed all hope, took away all striving, reduced to ashes the aspirations of all human striving!

We romanticize and fictionalize death. We see it as a sweet release provided by a loving Father calling us gently homeward. Not the earliest people of the Christian faith. They never saw death in any other light than as an enemy, a work of Satan, his worst work! That is why the apostle Paul says, "The last enemy to be destroyed is death" (1 Cor. 15:26). The *last* enemy! Last not only in the chronological sense of final, but last also in the cumulative sense of the most powerful. Death is the ultimate weapon of the evil one. And that is exactly what Hebrews 2:14 says, that Jesus partook of flesh and blood, became man, entered into death, "that through death *he might destroy him who has the power of death, that is, the devil.*"

New Testament Demonology

The New Testament will remain forever a closed book for you until and unless you recognize that it is saturated from beginning to end by demonology, by the conviction that Satan is the god of this world, the world ruler of this present darkness, the one who controls this present age and thus renders it evil. He manifests his malignant will through suffering and sickness, through hunger and deprivation, and sets his final seal on the futility of human existence by capturing all the sons of men with the weapon of death, of extinction.

This saturation of the New Testament by the belief in demonology, seen in the above passages, directly and explicitly, also saturates the fabric of the New Testament in a less direct, more ambiguous way. Once we have become sensitized to the dramatic dimensions of demonology, then suddenly many minor, more obscure passages, spring to light and explain themselves. For example, the demonology of that day believed that Satan's power was greatest in the hours of night. In the night hours the sons of darkness were at their zenith, and when the dawn broke their power slightly waned. This helps us to understand the otherwise inexplicable remark of Jesus when the forces of the crucifixion begin to close in on him. As he is arrested he says that this is the hour "of the power of darkness" (Luke 22:53). And that same demonology suddenly makes us aware of why it is that Peter begins to weep when the cock crows. During the night the devil was even more powerful, but when the dawn breaks and the cock crows, Peter returns to himself and realizes in full what he has done by denying Jesus.

The demonology of the New Testament is reflected in many other details which we ordinarily slide over easily. The people of that time were convinced that evil spirits resided in stagnant water, in fetid pools unfit to drink. But the evil one was not active in flowing streams, in fresh and sparkling water, and it was in running water, in the sweet stream of the Jordan that John was baptizing, for it was only there, in that kind of water, that Satan was not active. The people of that day were convinced that the powers of darkness were not only most active in the night-time hours, but they were also most active in specific daytime locales as well, daytime locales identified with death, corruption, and decay, places such as tomb areas and cemeteries. It is no coincidence that the man who is held in bondage by the demons, Mark 5:2f, lives "among the tombs."

Demonology affects and infects all the areas of New Testament thought and leads directly into that other area of New Testament emphasis, eschatology. Eschatology is the belief in the end of the world, the conclusion of the present age, the close of human existence as we know it now. The conviction that the present age is evil produces the hope that the future age will be cleansed. These are the twin blades of a scissors—one making sense out of the other, one meaningless without the other. There would be no need, no reason, to look for a new heaven and a new earth if the present heaven and earth were clean, if they were of God. But because this world is not clean and of God but is instead ruled over by Satan, the New Testament goes on to proclaim the future kingdom of God, the restoration of his rule, the end of Satan's reign, the coming of a new cosmos.

Practically every page of the New Testament breathes this powerful hope of future renewal, the time when Satan's rule shall be ended and God's reign renewed. The oldest extant pieces of literature in the New Testament, 1 and 2 Thessalonians, have this subject as their primary emphasis—the return of Jesus and the destruction of the evil one. His counterattack, his attempt to hold onto his usurped kingdom, will not succeed, and the day is coming when the devil shall be cast down and the fallen cosmos liberated!

Mark 13 and Matthew 24 also express this demonological-eschatological conviction. In Mark 13 Jesus looks forward to that final hour. He sees the approaching hour of tribulation, a time of suffering unparalleled in all of human existence: "For in those days there will be such tribulation as has not been from the beginning of the creation which God created until now, and never will be" (Mark 13:19). Why unparalleled tribulation? Because never before has the enemy been so great. Satan himself, the world-rulers of this present darkness, the spiritual host of wickedness must be shattered and shaken. And shaken they will be! He goes on to insist that "the powers in the heaven will be shaken" (Mark 13:25); there will be cosmic upheaval, for the structures of the world will be thrown down and destroyed before they can be made new. "The sun will be darkened and the moon will not give its light, and the stars will be falling from heaven." (Mark 13:24).

This is the thought echoed by Paul in 1 Corinthians 7:29, 31. Paul begins by insisting that "the time has grown very short." We are living in the final hours, and the "form of this world is passing away." The form, the structure of government, the world itself is about to go through a wrenching renewal. Paul thinks marriage is unwise. How foolish to bring children into a world exposed to the death-throes of Satan! Why bear children into a world about to be shaken? Paul continues his argument, "The time has grown very short; from now on let those who have wives live as though they had none." That is a thought shared fully by Jesus. He too, looking at the final hour, says, "Alas for those who are with child and for those who give suck in those days! For great distress shall be upon the earth. . . ." (Luke 21:23).

There shall be great distress on the earth, for the earth itself is being stripped of all control as satanic power is peeled off, and as Satan fights a losing battle to retain control. But God shall win the battle and the world itself will be set free, renewed, "born again." Paul speaks of the creation itself eagerly looking forward, yearning for the end, the time of release and renewal. "For the creation waits with eager longing . . . because the creation itself will be set free from its bondage to decay and obtain the glorious liberty of the children of God" (Rom. 8:19-21). And then, blunt as always, Paul actually uses the language of labor pains, of physical renewal, to describe the agony of the cosmos: ". . . the whole creation has been groaning in travail together until now" (Rom. 8:22).

A war is going on! Cosmic war! Jesus is the divine invader sent by God to shatter the strengths of Satan. In that light, the whole ministry of Jesus unrolls. Jesus has one purpose—to defeat Satan. He takes seriously the strength of the enemy. And this fact sheds light on the parties or sects with whom Jesus identifies. Suddenly, taking demonology seriously, we can see why Jesus on the one hand has nothing to do with the Sadducees, and why, on the other hand, he begins very close to the Pharisees only later to disown them.

With the *Sadducees* Jesus can have no fellowship. They are the "Greek" Jews, heirs of the group from the days of Antiochus Epiphanes who let their Jewish convictions lapse and took up instead Greek philosophy. The Sadducees, philosophically orientated to Greek thought, had given up all belief in the reality of Satan. They recognized that the doctrine of Satan is philosophically naive. It did not and it does not answer all the philosophical questions. Why did God create Satan in the first place? Why did God create Satan in such a way that he could fall, could rebel? Why does God tolerate his continued existence? When did Satan fall? Before the world began, or in the time of Antiochus Epiphanes?

As we described in the previous chapter, Jewish thought never answered any of those questions. It was not even able to decide when Satan fell because the doctrine of Satan was not a philosophical theorem at all. It was not an attempt to answer all philosophical questions. Philosophically it was naive. The aim of the doctrine of Satan was an attempt to hold on to belief in a good God in the middle of great suffering.

The Jew, living in the horrendous agony inflicted by Antiochus Epiphanes had one of two choices. Either the suffering he saw came from God, or it didn't! And what the doctrine of Satan was saying was a shout of faith. It was the insistence that whenever Satan fell, whyever he fell, these were not the important things. The important thing was that he, not God, was the source of all suffering. The doctrine of Satan was the shout raised out of adversity that the abortions of justice and the miscarriages of fairplay were not to be traced back to God but to the enemy of God. Why he fell, why he continued were not the central issues. Indeed, those issues were not even treated. One thing alone the belief in Satan affirmed, and that was that unfair suffering and enormous pain were incompatible with the conviction that God was just and fair and God loved his people.

Thus the suffering *had* to come from elsewhere. Where else? Satan! That is all the doctrine spoke to. It proclaimed continuing faith in the goodness of God in the middle of trial. All other philosophical issues were not treated. But the Sadducees were Greek in thought. And when they saw the naivete of the doctrine of Satan, they rejected the entire doctrine, refusing to believe at all in the reality of spirits (Acts 23:8). With them, therefore, Jesus could have no fellowship.

One of the striking truths of synoptic thought is that whenever someone is testing Jesus, trying to trap him, trying to ensnare him with a trick question, trying to hold Jesus up to ridicule, that someone is a Sadducee (see for example, Matt. 22:23f. and parallels). They did not believe in Satan. Jesus did. And thus no fellowship was possible.

The *Pharisees* fell into another caste. They were the "Jewish" Jews who had stood firm against Antiochus Epiphanes and had embraced Jewish tradition. Looking at the suffering of that hour they had come out of persecution with a belief in Satan. Thus Jesus, who has no fellowship with the Sadducees, establishes fellowship with the Pharisees. He sees a kinship, a oneness with them which he cannot have with the Sadducees.

There is a series of New Testament verses that shows Jesus identifying with the Pharisees. In Luke 14:1f. Jesus actually eats with the Pharisees. An extraordinary event when one remembers that there were no snack bars in ancient Israel. One did not eat with just anyone. Eating was no casual thing. To eat with someone meant to identify with them. There are two strong drives in man—one to reproduce, the other for self-preservation, food and sex. And both are private. You would no more invite a stranger into your dining room than you would into your bedroom. Just as sex united people, so did eating together. And Jesus eats with the Pharisees, identifies with them, sees them as co-believers in the reality of Satan, for their sons, like unto himself, cast out demons (Matt. 12:27).

Jesus sees the Pharisees as partners, members of

Satan in the New Testament

the household of God, united with him in the struggle against Satan. That is the only intelligent way one can interpret the three parables of Luke 15. In Luke 14:1f., we see Jesus eating with the Pharisees and identifying with them. They are his friends. And then Luke 15 begins with Jesus eating with tax collectors and sinners—and the Pharisees are aghast. How can Jesus identify with *them?* To allay their fears and put to rest their doubts, Jesus tells the three famous parables of the lost coin, the lost sheep, and the runaway prodigal son. There is a double emphasis to these three stories. On the one hand, there is Jesus' explanation as to why he eats with sinners. They too are children of God. God yearns for them, seeks them out, tries to rescue them. That emphasis is self-evident and needs no elaboration. But note the other emphasis, far more subtle, but perhaps even more important when one recognizes that it is the consternation of the Pharisee that precipitates those three stories. Each of the three stories includes a reference to some who need no repentance. There are other coins that were not lost. There were 99 sheep who did not have to be sought out. There is an elder brother who never strayed away. The context leaves no doubt that Jesus is referring to the Pharisees. He sees them as loyal children of God, firm in the faith, never having strayed. The parables are a double-edged attempt to explain why he can have fellowship not only with them but also with sinners. He has fellowship with the Pharisees because they are sons of the household, and he seeks out the lost because they are strayed sons.

And just as Jesus embraces and endorses the Pharisees, so also they respond in like manner. Luke 13:31 makes it clear that Jesus has friends within the

Pharisee circles. When his life is threatened by Herod they come and warn him (Luke 13:31).

That is the way it is in the early part of Jesus' ministry. While he cannot have fellowship with the Sadducees who have given up all belief in the reality of Satan, he can and does unite with the Pharisees who recognize him as one of their own, eat with him, and warn him of impending danger. But as the ministry of Jesus progresses, the issues become more clear, and a new dramatically altered relationship with the Pharisees emerges.

It becomes clear that while the Pharisees take Satan seriously, they certainly do not take him as seriously as does Jesus. To understand this, one must return anew to the days of Antiochus Epiphanes. In that dark hour of persecution, not only were the Essenes convinced that this world was under the power of the devil, but the Pharisees apparently accepted this too. They believed that the world was separated from God, exposed to Satan who ruled the world. But this pessimistic view of the world was lessened by later events. Antiochus Epiphanes was successfully resisted. The Maccabees won in their revolt against the Greeks.

For a short span of about 80 years, from about 143 B.C. to 63 B.C., the Jews regained their freedom. This was the age of the Hasmonean dynasty, the first time since Jerusalem fell to the Babylonians more than 400 years earlier that the Jews were a free people. Certainly that brief span of freedom was short-lived and marred by internal dissension, graft, collusion, and corruption, followed by enslavement under the Romans. But that did not alter the fact that, even if briefly, freedom *had* been won by the people of God. The world could not be *entirely* under the power of Satan or else the Jewish patriots,

Satan in the New Testament

the people of God, would never have won any freedom at all.

In this way a modified demonology came into being among the Pharisees. They continued to believe in the reality of Satan, but they did not see him as the omnipotent, irresistible ruler of the present hour. He was real, he was lethal, but he could be resisted. Man in his might, if he used the armor of God, could by his own efforts hold Satan at bay. This is how the Pharisees saw the law—as a weapon that could be used to hold off Satan. If a person kept all the regulations and minutiae of the law, there would be no opening through which Satan could seize him. That is why the Pharisees put such inordinate stress on regulations regarding clean and unclean, why they scoured cups, strained drinking water, exegeted and applied all the commandments of the law. They were convinced that if they were entirely faithful to the commandments of God they could, by their efforts, withstand the assault of the evil one. Indeed, they went so far as to insist that even Rome itself would topple and lose its grip if Israel would be faithful to the law. There is a well known and widespread statement that if Israel would perfectly keep the law for three consecutive sabbaths the kingdom of God would come.

In short, then, the Pharisees believed in the reality of Satan. But they also believed in man's innate ability to withstand the evil one. Thus, they concluded, if anyone did fall under the power of the devil, it was that person's own fault. That was why the Pharisees were inclined to look on the demon-possessed person not as supremely unfortunate but rather as supremely evil—he had sold his soul to the devil! This explains why the Pharisees were inclined to look on those who suffered as evil people. Why did they suffer? Because they had spurned God, identified with Satan, and thus incurred the wrath of God. The Pharisees, while they took Satan seriously, did not see him as the ruler of this world able at ease to invade anyone, even against the person's will, and hold that person in bondage. They had a view of Satan, but it was a relatively low view. They did not, for example, see the powers of darkness as welded together into one lethal foe. On the contrary, they had a fragmented concept of the powers of darkness, believing that those demonic forces lacked cohesiveness, that one demon could be used against another. This is behind their accusation of Jesus that it was by the "prince of demons he casts out demons" (Mark 3:22).

Jesus becomes aware that while he and the Pharisees talk about the reality of the devil, they mean different things by that reality. For them, Satan and his forces are disunited. One can be used against another. And they are weak; they can be resisted by man's personal diligence, and the person who does end up in their grip is one who brought it on himself.

In direct opposition to that view, Jesus eventually must break with the Pharisees. He insists that Satan's power is not divided. There is no group of independent unrelated fratricidal demons, one working against the other. On the contrary, he insists, Satan's hordes are welded together into a lethal kingdom—one cannot throw out another (Mark 13:23-26). In direct opposition to them, Jesus looks on the demoniac, the one invaded by demons, not as a supremely evil man who sold his soul to the devil, but rather as a supremely unfortunate person who has been captured even against his will. Thus Jesus has compassion on the demoniacs and sets them free.

In direct opposition to the Pharisaic view that suffering is a sign of sin and God's punishment—the view that if a man is lowly and down it is ample evidence that he has identified with the powers of darkness—Jesus points to the lowly injured person lying in the ditch and insists that that man is to be helped, to be ministered unto. In the parable of the Good Samaritan the two who walk by the injured man are a Levite and a priest, administrators of Old Testamen religion. Jesus tells the parable not to indicate that that Levite and priest are untrue to their religion. On the contrary, they *are* true to that religion. The Old Testament principle of retribution insisted that if a man were good he would be rewarded and if he were evil he would be punished. The man was lying in the ditch, suffering. Thus he was being punished. To help him was to oppose the will of God. And Jesus, in direct opposition, demands compassion and intervention.

In contrast to the principle of retribution that insists you can measure a man's piety by looking at the blessings he has accumulated, Jesus thunders in Luke 6:20f. that the exact opposite is true. If you live in a world under the power of Satan, the only way you can prosper is by identifying with Satan. Or conversely, if you side with God in opposition to Satan who rules the world, the only possible end result is suffering. Thus Jesus insists that it is the elect of God who are exposed to hunger, the work of the devil. If a man hungers, it is clear from the fact of his suffering that he is God's child: "Blessed are you that hunger now, for you shall be satisfied" (Luke 6:21). In the same way, if one is poor, deprived of the world's goods, then it is clear that that poor person has been spied out by Satan, the ruler of the world, and all the goods and wealth that Satan controls will be denied to that person.

Poverty is a sign not of God's judgment but of Satan's attack on the elect: "Blessed are you poor, for yours is the kingdom of God" (Luke 6:20). But Jesus goes even farther, saying not only the negative —that you will suffer in a world ruled by Satan if you side with God—but saying the positive as well— that if you side with Satan you will get rich. This view explains Luke 6:24, 25: "But woe to you that are rich . . . woe to you that are full now . . . woe to you that laugh now." This point of view, that Satan is in control of this world and thus heaps blessings on those who identify with him, rests behind the parable of the rich man and Lazarus. The two die and poor Lazarus goes to Abraham's bosom, but the rich man goes into the flames of torment. Not a single word has been said about their spiritual condition—not a single word *has* to be said. For it is clear to Jesus, as he already stated in the Luke 6 passages, that if a man is evil, has identified with Satan, he will be rich now; but if he sides with God in a world alienated from God he will be poor and will suffer, for Satan will attack him.

When this fundamental difference between Jesus and the Pharisees emerges and becomes clear we find the key to the dramatic change between Jesus and the Pharisees' relationship. At first, as we saw, he identifies with them. But as his ministry unrolls, it becomes clear to him that while they take Satan seriously, they do not take Satan as seriously as he does. They are foolish enough to believe that Satan can be resisted by man's efforts alone. They are foolish enough to believe that it is only the man who embraces evil who falls victim to Satan. Their view of Satan is too small. Not only too small, dangerous. They are creating a false sense of security. By underestimating the power of the enemy, they are breeding a false sense of confidence. They are endangering men's spiritual security by fostering the illusion that Satan can be held at bay by man's efforts. They are in danger of strengthening the power of Satan by blithely asserting that Satan can be resisted.

That is why Jesus eventually turns on his former friends and lashes out at them with the most vociferous language of the entire New Testament, the seven scathing woes of Matthew 23. "Woe to you, scribes and Pharisees, hypocrites! because you shut the kingdom of heaven against men . . . woe to you, scribes and Pharisees, hypocrites! for you traverse sea and land to make a single proselyte, and when he becomes a proselyte you make him twice as much a child of hell as yourselves" (Matt. 23:13-15). Because their view of Satan is too small, and as Jesus grows to see that, he breaks fellowship with the Pharisees and denounces them.

IV

Jesus in Conflict with Satan

We have, in this discussion, introduced without emphasizing it, another motif which must be explored—and that is the growth of Jesus. For those of us who take the incarnation seriously and believe that Jesus was true man, we must believe precisely that—that Jesus became *true* man! One must take a passage such as Luke 2:52 literally and seriously. Luke insists that as Jesus grew up, he "increased in wisdom and in stature." That is, just as his body expanded and grew, so also his comprehension, his mind, matured and expanded and grew.

Jesus' Self-understanding

We have already insisted that the virgin birth stories and the story of the twelve-year old Jesus in the temple must be taken seriously. From the outset, he saw himself as the one sent by God, the divine redeemer. But while he saw his overall destiny in advance, he did not see the details of that destiny clearly at the outset. He grew in wisdom and in stature. Just as Jesus' attitude toward the Pharisees was subject to alteration as he grew, so also Jesus' attitude toward his whole ministry grew. He saw himself as God's Son, the virgin birth and temple story insist on that, but what was God's Son to do? *That* question unfolds only gradually. That is why Jesus did *nothing* for the first thirty years of his known life! The first gospel gives us no hint, no word, of his early years. Why not? Because there is no word to be given. Jesus himself was waiting for some further insight or revelation, growing gradually into a comprehension of God's purposes.

That signal from God comes, apparently, in the ministry of John the Baptist. As that eschatological figure explodes on the scene with his message of the coming kingdom of God, Jesus is stirred, moved of the Spirit. He goes forth, is baptized—and then his destiny is affirmed. The voice from heaven speaks *to him* as he emerges from the water (note Mark 1:11, in contrast to Matt. 3:17—in Matthew, the voice from heaven speaks in the third person identifying Jesus to others as the Son of God, "This is my beloved son." But in Mark, the voice speaks in the second person, to Jesus himself. To Jesus the voice says, "You are my beloved Son").

In the preaching and the practice of John the Baptist Jesus receives the further revelation from God that the time has come to begin. He is the Son of God who has come to overthrow the powers of the devil. That no doubt is why he went to be baptized by John. Believing that the final act of cosmic liberation was to begin, and that he was the key or central figure in that battle with Satan, he was the one who would be the prime target for Satan's counter-attack. Thus he goes to receive the baptism, the shielding off of the wrath which was to come. As the

Jesus in Conflict with Satan 73

servant-son of God he would be attacked. And the baptism of John was the immunization against that attack.

And so he goes to be baptized, to be exempted from satanic trial, and immediately after the baptism he is attacked in the wilderness. The temptation follows the baptism. This is the first major crisis in the life of Jesus. He took Satan seriously, far more seriously than those about him, the Sadducees and Pharisees, but not seriously enough. For he thought Satan could be held off through baptism. But he could not be so held off. Jesus must revise upwards his estimate of satanic power, an upward revision that continues on later in his life.

The New Testament takes seriously the conviction that this world is enslaved under Satan who causes all suffering and woe, and Jesus is the one sent by God to destroy the devil and usher in the kingdom of God. In that vein the earliest writings about Jesus unfold. The gospel of Mark begins, in its very first sentence, by identifying Jesus as "the son of God." Not merely an itinerant evangelist, a barefooted son of Joseph walking across the eastland plains, but the Son of God. Divine invader. The declaration of war! And that is how the powers of darkness see him. When he appears, the hosts of darkness cringe and cry out, "What have you to do with us, Jesus of Nazareth? Have you come to destroy us? I know who you are, the Holy One of God!" (Mark 1:24). With that cunning insight reserved unto powers of darkness alone (Jesus in Luke 16:8 mentions that the powers of darkness seem to have greater intelligence than the elect of God, "the sons of this world are wiser in this generation than the sons of light"), the powers of darkness have seen what the elect have not seen—that Jesus is the Holy

One of God come to destroy them! They knew that the counterattack against Jesus had already begun. No sooner had he been baptized by John in the Jordan than the temptation began.

Incidentally, one must emphasize that the Greek word *peirazo* or *peirasmos*, usually translated temptation, has a broader meaning than temptation. *Peirasmos* can be translated temptation, that is, some in-internal movement toward evil, some fleeting moment of doubt and personal trouble. Or it can equally well be translated attack, as an external attack on a person quite independent of any internal wrestlings. And there can be no doubt that this is the way Mark speaks of the "temptation" of Jesus. It is not a "temptation" at all. Not one single word is said here about any internal doubt or wrestling by Jesus. On the contrary, it says simply that he is attacked by Satan. And notice, also, how briefly the attack is described. Only one and one-half verses in Mark 1. To elaborate on the attack, to stretch it out, to let it be prolonged, would be to emphasize the strength of Satan, his staying power, his continuing ability to plague Jesus.

But Mark is seeking to emphasize not the staying power of Satan but the superiority of Jesus, and thus comes the attack, and almost immediately its ending. And, Satan's attack having been rebuffed, Jesus can go on to answer the question of the demons. They asked, "Have you come to destroy us?" and the answer comes in the very next verse, Mark 1:25. It says that Jesus "rebuked" the evil spirit and said, "Be silent!"

Unfortunately both words are mild translations of powerful Greek verbs. What the Greek text literally says is not simply that Jesus "rebuked" or chided the evil force, but that he lashed out. He literally attacked the evil force. And the word translated "Be silent!" says, literally, that he throttled or strangled or choked off the demonic force!

That is the answer Jesus gives to the question of the demonic horde, "Have you come to destroy us?" The answer is a resounding *yes* as he lashes out and strangles the evil forces holding the poor demoniac in bondage. Having done it in deed, Jesus says it in word. In Mark 3:27 he insists that his purpose in coming is to bind the strong man (Satan) and plunder his house (set at liberty those who are oppressed).

In this way the entire Gospel of Mark unfolds. We who have grown up in the church and have listened to the gospel read and preached every week often blur together the distinctive emphases of the different gospels. We may miss the peculiar thrust of each one. We may not note that Mark probably the oldest of the four gospels, has little to report on what Jesus *says,* but a great deal to report on what Jesus *does.* Not until the later gospels Matthew and Luke do the great words of Jesus move to the fore. Matthew includes the extended Sermon on the Mount. Luke narrates the many famous parables. There is a minimum of preaching, of words by Jesus, in Mark. Instead, Mark concentrates on the works of Jesus, the miracles. If you divide the Gospel of Mark into two columns, putting everything into one column that deals with miracle either directly or indirectly, and everything left over into another column, you will see that 60 to 70 percent of Mark concentrates on the *miracles* of Jesus.

The Miracles of Jesus

These miracles are understood from within the framework of his battle with Satan. As we have already seen when we examined Luke 13:16 and 2 Corinthians 12:7, both Jesus and Paul trace illness back to Satan. And thus the miracles of healing are to be seen as slashing attacks by Jesus on the powers of darkness. Jesus attacks not only the person of the demons but also their works. The number one miracle of the synoptic gospels in terms of numerical frequency, the miracle which takes place more often than any other, is the miracle of exorcism, of casting out of demons. Its statistical superiority is evidence enough of its theological importance. Jesus has come to destroy the devil, and that means he must attack the person of the demons, the host of wickedness. Thus Mark 1:24f. is typical of the entire Gospel of Mark, as Jesus slashes out and strangles the evil forces. He attacks their person.

1. The Problem of Sickness

He not only attacks their person, he attacks their works. He undoes their damage. The devil causes sickness, and Jesus heals the sick. The miracles of healing are part of the same worldview that produced the exorcisms. In the deepest sense, the person of the demons and the work of the demons is inseparable. A united campaign must be waged against them. Thus Jesus heals as well as exorcises. Luke 4:38-39 is an extraordinarily significant passage from this point of view. Jesus enters into Simon Peter's house and finds Peter's mother-in-law ill with a fever and Luke goes on to insist that Jesus "rebuked" the fever. Precisely the same language is used on the fever as is used on the demon. If there is any meaning to language at all, if words are to be used as clues to thought, then the only conclusion possible is that Jesus uses the same word in addressing a fever as he does in addressing a demon because he sees a lethal unity between sickness and Satan.

And he heals. Luke 7:21 is an interesting passage from this point of view. The Revised Standard Version translates, "In that hour he cured many of diseases and plagues and evil spirits." And that is a legitimate translation. But there is another possible way the verse or thought can be translated. The RSV translation implies a separateness of diseases, and plagues, and evil spirits; it implies that there is no relationship between these things. But the Greek word *mastix*, plague, can equally well be translated whip or weapon. With that translation, an entirely different sense emerges. These three things are not numerically distinct, but instead disease is one of the weapons evil spirits use. That is, as Jesus overcomes sickness, he is shattering satanic power. In that vein one can make sense out of the next set of verses.

John the Baptist is sitting in prison. He sends word to Jesus to be assured that Jesus is the divine redeemer, the one sent by God to destroy the devil and bring in the kingdom. To reassure John and give him his requested answer, Jesus says, "Go and tell John what you have seen and heard: the blind receive their sight, the lame walk, lepers are cleansed, and the deaf hear, the dead are raised up, the poor have good news preached to them." That is the answer to John's question. Is Jesus the one sent by God to bring in the kingdom and end satanic oppression? Certainly! The evidence is that he is breaking down and rendering useless the demonic weapon of sickness.

The miracles of healing, then, are evidences of the power of Jesus, the story of his conquest of Satan. Today there are still those who insist that a view which sees sickness as a work of Satan is medieval, fraught with superstition, not to be accorded credulity in our enlightened age. We are now a mature people far advanced beyond this earlier adolescence of our race that saw sickness as demonic. We are told that we cannot accept sickness as the work of evil spirits, because today we know that viruses and germs, not demonic spirits, cause disease.

The biblical view that sickness is a work of the devil is held up to ridicule and scorn, despised as obscurantism, rejected as out-dated. Where do we go when we have a headache? To the pastor for prayer or to the pharmacist for aspirin? The answer is self-evident, and the implication is enormous. We are told that our taking of aspirin is evidence enough that we no longer see disease as theological, but as scientific-medical. Now certainly there is a truth to that. Every time we have a toothache we don't cry out that Satan is stabbing us in the molars. Certainly we must take serious stock of the advances of medical technology. But even when full account is taken of the marvels of modern medicine, the mystery remains.

I am not at all positive that we really have said or seen anything significant simply because we can isolate a death-dealing virus under a microscope or in a laboratory culture. I am not really convinced that we have truly spoken to the profound problem of human pain and sickness simply because we can give a Greek or a Latin name to the disease that destroys our children and wipes away our hopes and ravages our loved ones. There is an element of mysterious malignant evil in the fact of human sickness. And Jesus, with the Jews of old, looked at the staggering menace of widespread disease. He did not psychologize or philosophize or seek to explain in medical jargon what was taking place—*he healed!* He ripped through the web of pseudo-sophistication that assumes a thing named is therefore tamed, and *he healed!*

In Jesus' miracles of healing, there emerges not essentially a comprehension of the nature of sickness, but a view of God—a God who identifies with us in our suffering and pain and works to overcome that suffering and pain. Wherever human life is infected and poisoned, the power of Jesus operates to set people free. The essential emphasis is not on sickness or Satan at all, but on the overwhelming comforting superiority of Jesus who is greater than every foe we shall ever face.

2. The Problem of Hunger

Hunger too is a work of the devil. And therefore, alongside the miracles of healing are the miracles of feeding. So significant is the story of the feeding of the 5000 that it is the only miracle story told in all four gospels. When God was in control, before the fall of Satan, there was food in abundance. Man could walk in the cool of the garden in fellowship with the Father and he could echo the divine statement, "It is good . . . it is good." There was food in abundance in the garden of Eden.

But now that Satan has seized control, there is no more abundance, but deprivation, want, famine, hunger. The nature miracles of Jesus—the stilling of the storms, the cursing of the barren fig tree, the draught of many fishes, the multiplication of the bread—are all signs that the new cosmos is on the way. Even as the Spirit of God had earlier brought order out of chaos, so also now in the life of Jesus all things were being made new, set in order, and hunger was being overcome. Eden was being restored! Negatively, the hostile elements of nature are met and mastered. Men went down to the sea in ships to gather fish to feed their families, and instead they found their lives in jeopardy. Storm at sea! And Jesus stills the storms, calms the seas. The negative forces of nature are neutralized.

It is no accident of language that precisely the same word used on the demon in Mark 1:24, "rebuke," is also used on the fever of Peter's mother-in-law, Luke 3:39, but it is used as well on the raging sea. In Mark 4:39f. Jesus wakes to the worried pleas of his disciples and he "rebukes" the sea and says, "Be still!" to the storm. Precisely the same words he uses on the person of the demons because he sees the storms and all the ravages of nature, as the works of the demons. That which is negative, sterile, barren, denying the fulness of God, must be excised and erased. So Jesus curses the barren fig tree. It is not bearing fruit. It is not feeding God's children. So it must go. And this, despite the fact that it is not the season for figs! In God's goodness, there is no time for barrenness and deprivation.

Negatively he stills the storms and curses the barren tree; positively he not only neutralizes the negative aspect of nature, he also restores its bounty. Several small loaves and a multitude eats. Several tiny fish, and a multitude eats. And when all have eaten their fill an abundance is left over, 12 baskets full, enough for every tribe of Israel to have surplus. *That* is what the prodigal goodness of God intended. Plenty, abundance! The sea is stilled, but that does not end the miracles of the sea. Jesus goes on to tell the disciples to cast out their net after a fruitless night of fishing, and they catch so many fish that the boat starts to sink, the nets begin to break. *That* is what the prodigal goodness of God intended. Plenty, abundance! The nature miracles assume form and substance only when they are taken seriously against the demonology of that day. They are attacks on Satan, the ending of the diabolical deprivation hurled against man.

There are those who tell us today that such a view is archaic, antiquated, indefensible in an enlightened age that has developed the green revolution, agricultural science, and modern fertilizers. There are those who tell us that hunger is no longer to be superstitiously seen as a religious problem, but is purely a transportation problem of supply and demand, of distributing the surplus of one area to the needy of another.

I am not sure of the accuracy of such easy solutions. I have difficulty in sloughing off the tragedy of widespread famine as purely a technological trouble. There is something demonic about the fact that large segments of the world's people go to bed hungry every night. I have lived in Africa and seen bloated bellies in the last stages of protein starvation. With aching eyes and troubled heart I have buried little schoolboys in Africa and have been driven to my knees by that awesome question, "Why, O Lord why?"

The New Testament does not deal in a dilettantish way with international economics or transportation problems as if they were philosophical issues to be bantered over at our ease. The New Testament strips away all the verbiage of a too-talkative do-nothing generation and shouts, "Hunger is evil, it is of the devil!" Jesus heals and Jesus feeds the multitudes. What emerges out of those miracle stories of nature being neutralized and restored is not the skeleton of a new social program, not the embryo of a foodstamp plan. What does emerge is a vision of God concerned about his creation. What emerges is the powerful picture of suffering and hunger as real forces. But there also emerges an even more powerful picture of God who has identified with us in our want and shortages, fighting on our behalf, ending our ills and setting us free and ushering us into the bliss of his presence.

3. The Problem of Death

But the one major weapon of the devil is not sickness or hunger, but death. Those who weep for want of food may one day hear the hum of thresher's wheels. And those who waste because of illness may one day find a final cure. But for those who are dead, there is no hope. The final fact of the grave, the stillness of the tomb write *finis* to all human striving. If God is truly on our side, then death, the last great enemy, must be met and mastered.

And that is why the Gospel of John, having carefully considered the many miracles of Jesus, ends by reducing the many mighty works of Mark down to symbolic seven signs. Mark's continuing emphasis on the miracles of Jesus is both a strength and a weakness. It is a strength. The proliferation of many mighty deeds comes like one thunder clap after another to assert and affirm the superiority of Jesus. When one has finished reading Mark, one sits there with a slack-jawed eye-popping comprehension of the power of this Jesus. Every paragraph, nearly every sentence, brings another revelation of his awesome superiority and his power to beat down and master the enemy holding us in thralldom. But it is a weakness as well. So many miracles, undifferentiated, hurled one on top of the other, make it difficult for us to see the ascending significance of this

Jesus in Conflict with Satan 83

increasing attack on the entrenched powers of darkness. What *is* the primary contribution of Jesus? Where does the heart of his ministry lie? Is it only in the healing of diseases? Are those like Katherine Kuhlmann right when they concentrate almost exclusively on the abolition of illness. Was that the essential thrust of Jesus of Nazareth? Mark, with his many miracles, might lead one to that mistaken view.

But the Gospel of John goes back over the mighty works of Jesus. It eliminates many, organizes the rest, arranges them all in an ascending order of importance so that we can see the climax, the most essential. The flurries against sickness and disease, the feeding of the hungry, as vital as they are, are introductory to the great victory of Jesus, his triumph over death. Death must be beaten. Thus the final, the seventh, the major miracle of Jesus in the Gospel of John is the raising of Lazarus.

The organization in John provides the clue to the synoptics, for in the synoptics too the miracle of resurrection, the defeat of death, the shattering of the ultimate weapon of Satan is the essential element in the invasion of Jesus. He has come to destroy the devil and all his works and all his ways, and if that is to be accomplished, then the devil must be hit where he is strongest. His empire of death must be ended.

Now we must return to a thought we touched on earlier, the growth in Jesus' own understanding. As we saw, even though he took Satan seriously, far more so than did the Sadducees and even the Pharisees, he nonetheless had to revise upward his estimate and evaluation of Satan's power. He went to be baptized to receive the divine protection of that rite, thinking that by submission to that baptism he would be exempted from satanic counterattack. Such was not so. After the baptism came the attack. Satan was able to pierce through the protective mantle of baptism. Satan was able to counterattack. His fury was great.

This emphasis on the ability of Satan to counterattack permeates nearly all the words of Jesus. In one parable, for example (Luke 11:24-26), the ability of the demonic powers to strike back is the sole subject. He speaks of a demon being driven out only to return with seven other spirits more evil than the first one. This same emphasis on the ability of Satan to strike back shows up in that otherwise strange and incomprehensible word found in Matthew 11:11-15. Jesus here speaks of the greatness of John the Baptist, the harbinger of the kingdom of God, the first to announce that the reign of God was imminent. And then he goes on to insist that "From the days of John the Baptist until now the kingdom of God has suffered violence, and men of violence take it by force."

Unfortunately, that translation is a poor one. The text in Greek does not say that *"men"* of violence "take it" by force. The text says that *the violent ones fight back*. They use force. They resist the approach of the kingdom of God. Which violent ones? The overall context makes it clear that Jesus is speaking of the devil and the entrenched powers of evil. The words of John the Baptist, "The kingdom of God is at hand," were the declaration of war against Satan. The initial announcement, "The kingdom of God is coming" was the announcement that Satan's rule was ending, and they were thus resisting that advance of the kingdom. They were doing everything in their power to throw it back, to resist its coming.

In Luke 11:20 Jesus insists that the approach of the

Jesus in Conflict with Satan

kingdom of God is in direct proportion to the route of the demons: "But if it is by the finger of God that I cast out demons, then the kingdom of God has come upon you." The passage goes on to make clear that what is taking place is the destruction of Satan's power. The strong man is being assailed by one who is stronger (Luke 11:22). The devil will and does strike back. As the kingdom of God comes, as his own empire is threatened, Satan's wrath and fury increase because, as it says in Revelation 12:12, he knows that his time is short.

This striking-back of the evil one shows up in other parables and places as well. Read for example, the twin parables of Matthew 13:18-30. In these two stories Jesus speaks of the efforts of God to sow the seed being resisted by the enemy. On the one hand, the enemy tries to tear up the seed and, in the other parable, he plants weeds or tares among the seed. And Jesus, in Matthew 13:39, explicitly insists that the enemy is the devil, resisting the advance of God's rule.

This same emphasis on the ability of Satan to counterattack, to resist the advance of God's rule, is the key to unlocking many other verses in the New Testament as well. By way of illustration, Jesus says, in an almost incredible passage in Luke 12:49ff. "I came to cast fire upon the earth; and would that it were already kindled. . . . Do you think that I have come to give peace on earth? No, I tell you, but rather division." Strange words from the Prince of Peace! How should we understand them? As a desire of Jesus to cause suffering and pain and make woe mount up? Not at all. His entire ministry of alleviating pain and suffering demands that another answer be given. And that answer is not that he desires or wants suffering to take place. Not at all.

To Peter he says that he has prayed God to spare Peter tribulation. For himself, he cries out to the Father to take the cup of suffering away.

The Lord's Prayer

Nothing in the earliest strata of Christian teaching views suffering as something commendable, to be sought out and embraced. The suicidal drive for martyrdom, the embrace of pain and deprivation that characterized the later post-New Testament church, has no justification or responsive echoes in the New Testament. Jesus did not want suffering and pain. But he did see it as inevitable, necessary, unavoidable. To attack Satan meant to provoke counterattack. Before the kingdom of God could come, indeed, in order for it to come, the kingdom of Satan had to be broken. That is why he came not to bring peace but division and sword. Satan's realm was to be shattered, and Satan would fight back.

This point of view provides the key to the proper understanding of the Lord's prayer. Unfortunately, the way most of us have memorized it, we miss its true meaning.

Notice that the first petition after the hallowing of God's name is that God's kingdom come, his reign be extended to earth as it is even then practiced in heaven. "Thy kingdom come, thy will be done on earth as it is in heaven." That is a correct reflection of the apocalyptic view of the revolt of Satan, the fall of the heavenly council, as repeated in Revelation 12:7f. Revelation 12:7f. says, "War arose in heaven," but Michael and the loyal angels, fighting on God's behalf, were able to expel the rebels. They were defeated on high "and there was no longer any place for them in heaven. And the great dragon was thrown down . . . he was thrown down to the earth, and his angels were thrown down with him." How then are things above? Fine! Satan is no more on high, no longer a member of the heavenly council. Thus Revelation 12:12 can go on to shout, "Rejoice then, O heaven and you that dwell therein!" Certainly they can rejoice, because for them the devil is no longer a problem. But where did he go? He was thrown down to earth. Thus the same verse can go on to add, "But woe to you, O earth and sea, for the devil has come down to you in great wrath, because he knows that his time is short."

That is the background of Jesus' opening line in the prayer he taught us. He is imploring the Father that the expulsion or destruction of Satan on high be continued on earth. "Thy kingdom come, thy will be done *on earth as it is in heaven.*" Everything is alright upstairs. Satan has been thrown out after a great battle, and all is right in the heavenly areas. But now he is to be pursued. His reign on earth is to end, and his wrath is great because he knows that his time is short.

The prayer of Jesus continues (Matt. 6:9-13), "Give us this day our daily bread." Unfortunately, the Greek does not say that. There is no conceivable grammatical way that the Greek text can be twisted to make it say "daily bread." It *does* say, "Give us today the bread of tomorrow" as the footnote in most translations makes clear. What possible meaning should be given to receiving tomorrow's bread today? Again, the demonology of the New Testament infuses meaning into that phrase. The New Testament, as we have seen, insists that hunger is a work of the devil. But when Satan is destroyed, there will be bread in abundance, bread to overflowing. On the morrow, when Satan is destroyed, there will be bread. And Jesus has just requested the Father to destroy the devil, to end his rule on earth even as his revolt in heaven was quelled. But Satan is going to fight back and attack the elect of God. He will use every weapon at his disposal including hunger, to punish the elect.

And Jesus is simply saying that the mercies of God will reach forward, that we are free even now to ask, in the middle of the counterattack of the evil one, for God to give us some of the future abundance in the present hour that we might survive the final wrath of the evil one. Incidentally, the prayer that the bread of the morrow, the abundance of the future feast, might be shared even now, was fulfilled. It was fulfilled at that time in the feeding of the multitudes who tasted the abundance of God even in the midst of Satan's reign. And it is fulfilled now in the sacrament of the Lord's Table when the elect of God gather to taste the first fruits of the coming heavenly banquet. There is a forward look to holy communion, an anticipation of that great final feast when the devil is fully vanquished.

But the Lord's Prayer goes on. The kingdom has been asked for, Jesus has requested that God's rule be done on earth even as it is in heaven. The restoration of God's rule means the end of Satan's power, but he will fight to hold on. He will cause hunger, and the elect still need to be fed. But he will do more than cause hunger. He will attack in many and various ways. The next line of the prayer picks up that theme, "And lead us not into temptation, but deliver us from evil." Again, a very poor translation. The Greek word we translate as temptation is *peirasmos*, and we have already seen that the word has a double meaning. It may refer to internal trial or temptation, or it may refer to external attack by a vicious enemy. The latter meaning is indicated here. The New Testament itself dramatically insists that God does not test or tempt. Why then ask him not to lead us into temptation? This petition asks that when the devil strikes back, when his counterattack comes, that we be delivered from that attack. That is precisely what the next line says. It does *not* say "deliver from evil" but it does say "deliver us from the *evil one*."

The entire prayer of Jesus is demonologically-oriented, based on the conviction that this present world is not under God's rule but Satan's sway. The prayer asks that the rule of God come soon, and when it does, that the elect be sustained and cared for during the time of the devil's counterattack, that they be delivered out of the hand of the evil one. Incidentally, it is good to be reminded that the familiar ending, "For thine is the kingdom and power and glory forever" is not part of the oldest manuscripts. It is excluded from Matthew 6, for it does not belong there. God's kingdom and power and glory are not yet, but future, when Satan is destroyed.

All through his ministry Jesus respects and recognizes the lethal counterattacking power of Satan. But, to return to the theme of Jesus' personal growth, as great as is his respect for Satan's power, that respect is still not high enough in his early ministry and must be revised upwards, especially as that ministry moves to a close.

The Mission of the Disciples

Jesus believes that Satan causes sickness. And he heals. Jesus believes that Satan causes hunger. And he feeds the multitudes. Jesus believes that Satan causes death. And he raises the dead. Nonetheless, it appears that Jesus at the outset did not see the full dimensions or dramatic extent of Satan's power. That appears to be the point of Matthew 10:1f. This is a solemn moment. Jesus gathers his disciples together to send them out on a mission, a mission that is to be the final mission. In a solemn moment, Matthew 10:1-4, each one is named as the role is called.

Then, after each one has been identified, they are given their charge (Matt. 10:5-8). They are to go out on the briefest of missionary expeditions. Their itinerary is not world-wide, not at all inclusive. Instead, it is sharply truncated: "Go nowhere among the Gentiles, and enter no town of the Samaritans, but go rather to the lost sheep of the house of Israel." Their itinerary is abridged. Their ministry is not to be exhaustive, merely representative. Just a small portion of the world's population is to be visited.

And what are they to do? First, they are to announce that the kingdom of God is coming: "And preach as you go, saying 'The kingdom of heaven is at hand'" (Matt. 10:7). But they are not only to *announce* the kingdom of heaven; they are to bring it in. Jesus tells them that they are the ones who are to shatter Satan's grip. All the weapons of the evil one they are to destroy. "Heal the sick, raise the dead, cleanse lepers, cast out demons." They must announce that the reign of Satan is ending, the kingdom of God coming, and then bring that kingdom of God by ending the reign of Satan—overcome hunger, heal the sick, raise the dead, cast out the demons. Then comes the long warning that if they announce the kingdom of God and bring it closer they will also be subject to Satan's counterattack. "Behold, I send you out as sheep in the midst of wolves . . . Beware of men; for they will deliver you up . . . flog you" (Matt. 10:16-18). Jesus assures them, however, that they need not fear, for they will be sustained (Matt. 10:19) and their work will eventually succeed. For, despite the shortness of their journey, before that journey is ended the kingdom of God will arrive. "When they persecute you in one town, flee to the next; for truly I say to you, you will not have gone through all the towns of Israel, before the Son of man comes" (Matt. 10:23).

These verses are not obscure or unclear, but they are very uncomfortable. Their clear and literal sense is that the disciples will route Satan and lead to his toppling. As they cast out demons and raise the dead and heal the sick, they will bring about the end of Satan's reign. Jesus speaks about the appearance of the Son of man, his coming, as the consequence of the ministry of the disciples. Jesus expected to be transported on high and to return in triumph as a result of the ministry of the disciples, and not one word, either in this chapter or in the entire preceding synoptic narrative, has he spoken about even the possibility much less the necessity of his own death. Here he affirms that the end of the world will arrive without his having to die.

This is a low view of the power of Satan. It assumes that Satan's kingdom is but a house of cards. A blow here, a blow there, a concerted attack by the disciples, even though not broad geographically, will cause Satan's structure to topple. There is no grammatical way to get around that meaning. The attack of the disciples, although limited, will allow the coming of the Son of man.

The disciples go out, and they return. There is no end to Satan's empire. The foray has been unsuccessful. A gritty subsoil under the satanic empire has kept it from toppling. The efforts of the disciples were not enough. The kingdom of God did not come.

V

The One Who Conquers Death

Jesus must withdraw to think through the issues anew. And withdraw he does. In Matthew 11:11f., in those verses we have already examined, he speaks about the counterattack of Satan, the resistance of the violent ones subjecting the coming of the kingdom to violence. And then he withdraws, in isolation with his disciples, to the remote areas of Caesarea Philippi.

The Turning Point at Caesarea Philippi

At Caesarea Philippi Jesus comes to recognize that no efforts of the disciples will be sufficient to topple the satanic empire. No broadside attempts by them will cause Satan to crumble. He, Jesus, is the one who must do it! He is the one who must grapple with the most powerful weapon of Satan—death. At Caesarea Philippi, for the very first time, after the abortive attempt of the disciples to bring in the kingdom in Matthew 10, Jesus speaks of death for himself. *"From that time* [Caesarea Philippi, never earlier] Jesus began to show his disciples that he must go to Jerusalem and suffer many things from the elders and chief priests and scribes, and be killed, and on the third day be raised." Only after the failure of the disciples to bring in the kingdom does Jesus see the full dimensions of Satan's power. He himself must enter into death so that by entering into death he might destroy him who has the dominion of death, that is, the devil.

He resolves to die, not as an end, but as a means. On the third day he will be raised. He is the one—none other—who has the power to meet Satan at that critical point.

That he did not have such a view earlier is seen in Peter's reaction to the announcement of the impending death of Jesus. He explodes, "God forbid, Lord! This shall never happen to you" (Matt. 16:22). One can easily see the perplexity of Peter. He had just finished calling Jesus the Son of the living God and had been blessed for so identifying Jesus (Matt. 16:17). But Peter's problem was that he had a certain image of God. He had read the Old Testament, the only school book of the times. He learned that the Old Testament emphasizes that God is the source of all life; he cradles the seas and holds the mountains in his hands. It was God who breathed the breath of life into Adam. God is life, the source of all life. For Peter to believe that God, the source of all life, could die was an absurdity and an impossibility. And Peter had just identified Jesus as Son of God! *That* is the problem for Peter. He had just called Jesus Son of God! And now he heard that he, Jesus, was going to die. One can almost hear the wheels in Peter's head whirring as he says to himself, "Now wait just a minute, Jesus. Either you are what I have identified you as, and you cannot die.

The One Who Conquers Death 95

Or else you are going to die, and you are not the Son of God."

It was as simple—and as difficult—as that for Peter. Jesus was the Son of God—thus he could not die!

This passage makes clear that this was a crucial and a critical problem for Jesus as well as for Peter. All along he believed that he was God's Son, the divine redeemer. That he knew from the virgin birth stories heard from his mother and treasured from his youth. This he believed, as was evidenced by his insistence at age 12 that God was his Father.

That belief, however, that he was God's Son, had been challenged at least at one point of his life. Everything in his own personal circumstances seemed to indicate that the opposite was true. And that issue came to focus in the temptation scene as recorded by Matthew. Mark speaks of the temptation as not temptation at all, but rather as attack, as we have seen—an attack quickly repulsed. But Matthew preserves it in another way. Matthew sees Jesus as struggling internally. Struggling with what? The opening words of Satan in both of the first two temptations is critical: *"If you are* the Son of God. . . ."* (Matt. 4:3, 6). Obviously Jesus was wrestling with the contradiction between what he believed and what men could observe. He was the Son of God, yet he was hungry, had no bread, and God was the source of all bread, opening up his hand and feeding every living thing! If Jesus truly were God, why was he hungry? *"If you are* the Son of God, turn these stones into bread and eat!"

God was the answer to affliction and pain. God was above all human anguish and ill, incapable of death, for he was immortal and eternal. But Jesus appeared to have the markings of mortal man. If he truly were divine, he too should be immune from pain and suffering. "If you are the Son of God, throw yourself down" from the temple top, and you will bear no mortal consequence! Jesus, in those days in the wilderness alone with the devil, is wrestling with the astounding contradiction about what he believed himself to be—the Son of God—and what he was, an itinerant evangelist, poor, a son of a carpenter, apparently subject to deprivation and death.

But he overcame that temptation by reciting God's word. He overcame it, but did not quench or end it. It is a mistake to confine Jesus' temptation to a mere 40 days and 40 nights at the outset of his ministry as if temptation would never again reappear. On the contrary, the continuing aspect of Jesus' temptation —his temptation to doubt whether or not he is truly God's Son—is underlined by Luke's insistence that the devil "departed from him [Jesus] until an opportune time" (Luke 4:13).

That opportune time came at Caesarea Philippi. Peter sees the contradiction between what Jesus is, the Son of God, and what Jesus says he must do, go to Jerusalem and die. But Jesus sees that same contradiction. It is precisely because Peter puts in front of him the identical problem with which he wrestled in the wilderness earlier that both events close with the same words, "Get behind me, Satan!" (Matt. 16:23, also Matt. 4:10). They are the same words, because it is the same temptation. Earlier, he was being led to question whether or not he truly could be the Son of God.

Now he had announced that he was going to die —and the old temptation, now seen by Peter, returns with vengeance. How can the Son of God die? It is because earlier he did not expect to die that we can understand his statement in Matthew 10:23 that the end would come without any mention of his death, and why Peter's words evoke the same response as did the earlier slants of Satan.

At Caesarea Philippi Jesus at last came to the full appreciation and realization of the awesome powers of Satan. He realized that no other person, no other force, could dislodge Satan's kingdom. Jesus alone could shatter Satan's realm, but it would mean that Jesus had not merely to still storms and heal the sick and feed the hungry or send his disciples to do the same. He himself had to enter into death and destroy it. "Since therefore the children share in flesh and blood, he himself likewise partook of the same nature, that through death he might destroy him who has the power of death, that is, the devil" (Heb. 2:14). "The last enemy to be destroyed is death" (1 Cor. 15:26).

On this note the synoptic story draws to a close, not as the unfortunate story of a helpless man overwhelmed by forces he could not resist, not as the tragic somber story of an unfortunate man betrayed by a disciple, victim of a miscarriage of Roman justice, swept along by tides he could not resist.

To Jerusalem—and Victorious Death

How we have misunderstood and perverted this victory march of Jesus in some of our Lenten lamentations. Whenever we spend an undue time deploring the treachery of Judas, bemoaning his lack of loyalty to his Lord, whenever we piously beat our breasts and regret his traitorous act, we come perilously close to perverting the whole Gospel story. By weeping over the evil action of Iscariot we run the risk of making Judas the key figure in the unfolding drama. We suggest that if only he had been more loyal, less greedy, Jesus would not have so suffered. To even suggest that is to misunderstand the entire Passion narrative. Jesus was never helpless in the hands of Judas. It was he, Jesus, who here too was in total charge of the situation, master of every event, never victim but controller of the unfolding situation. The Gospel of John makes this dramatically clear. There, at the table, the night of the Last Supper, John 13:27 makes it abundantly clear that Judas does not move a muscle until Jesus orders him to go out. "What you are going to do, do quickly."

Pilate, second level Roman administrator, struts like a peacock trying to terrorize Jesus, tyrannize him, seeking to force him into submission by insisting, "Do you not know that I have power to release you, and power to crucify you?" (John 19:10). And Jesus turns on Pilate and makes his very blood run cold, frightening the poor vacillating man, dismissing him as a puppet, "You would have no power over me unless it were given you from above" (John 19:11). Those who bemoan the spastic convulsions and reverses of Pilate, those who make too much of his wavering oscillations, one moment declaring Jesus innocent only later to condemn him, are in serious danger of making Pilate, not Jesus, the central figure. Jesus, not Pilate, is master of the situation. Jesus died, not because Pilate is a spaghetti-spined weakling. Jesus died not because Judas is a traitor. Jesus died because he intended to die, in order to conquer death.

At Caesarea Philippi he recognized that Satan's realm and reign could not be ended until death was vanquished. And that is why he went to Jerusalem. Not to preach, but to die. The synoptic gospels make it clear that as soon as the issue was clearly seen at Caesarea Philippi, he immediately set his face like flint toward the unholy city of the prophets, Jerusalem. He went to Jerusalem not to preach but to die.

When he entered Jerusalem he was lauded and misunderstood. The word of his mighty deeds of the north had preceded him. They had heard of his awesome ability to still the storms, cast out the demons, raise the dead, and heal the sick. And these subjugated people, with the heavy boot of Caesar crushing their chest, looked to him as a political deliverer, a nationalistic hero. Surely if he could calm the surging seas he could also drive out Rome and give them liberty and independence. And thus they cheered him on the day of his arrival. Palm Sunday. They cut down palm branches and threw their robes in the road. In a paroxysm of joy and expectation they hailed him as a military deliverer, a son of David who had earlier beaten all enemies to their knees. They gave him a tumultuous welcome, a ticker-tape parade, the red carpet treatment. He could beat back the Romans as the Maccabees had earlier beaten back the Greeks.

But his kingship was not of this world. He had not come to Jerusalem to rally a revolt, or even to preach. He had come to die, and by dying conquer death. He had come to give his life as a ransom for many, to liberate the oppressed, to end the tyranny of Satan.

Thus, in direct opposition to the enthusiastic excitement his arrival had generated, he must do something to offset that popularity. He must find some means of goading the leaders of Jerusalem into accomplishing what he wished to accomplish—his death! And something he does. He antagonizes the religious leaders of the day, he cleanses the temple, he publicly proclaims them thieves and robbers and drives them out with a corded whip. Jesus the strong man is in charge, not victim but prime mover, marshalling into action the forces around him. He came to Jerusalem to die in order to conquer death, and die he will!

Unable to ignore him, the opposition moves. They arrest him. They bring him to trial. But they were forced to act precipitously. They do not have sufficient evidence to bring in a negative vedict. They try. They scheme. They hire false witnesses to come to court and lie against him. But they had been forced by Jesus to act quickly. They did not have sufficient time to coach the witnesses in their false testimony. In the middle of that testimony the stories of the liars conflict and a verdict is rendered impossible. Jesus will have to be released. But he does not intend to be released or exonerated. He has come to die!

When the stories of the false witnesses sag, Jesus provides from his own lips the needed evidence. He himself speaks the words that lead to his condemnation, and thus the high priest is able to say, "Why do we still need witnesses? You have heard his blasphemy. What is your decision? And they all condemned him as deserving death" (Mark 14:63-64). It is on his own testimony that he dies. Jesus is in charge of the situation.

Instead of being overwhelmed by the situation, a victim, a confused person confronted by unexpected opposition, the perfidy of a disciple and the weakness of a Roman administrator, Jesus is in total charge. He strides forward like a conqueror king approaching his throne. They beat him, they whip him, they make him carry his own cross. And under that crushing burden of wood and insult he stumbles and falls. And immediately the weeping women of Jerusalem reach out to mother him with their tears. But Jesus

The One Who Conquers Death

rejects their sobbing sentimentality. He rises up out of that blood-spattered dust, shoulders his cross, and marches forward to his death with the strength of such undiluted dimensions that even the Roman officer, standing at the foot of the cross, is astonished. A Roman centurion, in charge of 100 men, a tough non-commissioned officer, equivalent to a sergeant in the toughest fighting force the world had ever known, undoubtedly a brave man, probably scarred by the swords of other brave men, even this respecter of strength and power stands awed and amazed. He spoke those memorable words of admiration, "Truly this was the son of God!" (Mark 15:39).

That is the way Jesus died! Divine redeemer. Invader of the fallen planet. The one sent by God to destroy the devil and all his works and all his ways, to destroy sin, death, and the devil. He died that way because he did not see his death as the end, but as the new beginning. Never, not once, in the many times that he predicted his coming death, never did he fail to add those significant words, "and on the third day rise again!"

If the church were true to its Old Testament heritage, it would worship on Saturday, the Sabbath. If the cross were the center of Jesus' ministry, the church would worship on Friday, the day of the crucifixion. But the day of worship is not Friday or Saturday—it is Sunday, the Lord's day, the day of the resurrection. The resurrection of Jesus is the central affirmation of the Christian religion. The apostle Paul, ardently, unambiguously argues that the resurrection is the key, the central issue, the heart of the work of Christ. ". . . if Christ has not been raised, then our preaching is in vain and your faith is in vain. . . . If Christ has not been raised, your faith is futile and you are still in your sins. . . . But in fact

Christ has been raised from the dead" (1 Cor. 15:14, 17, 20).

His death was the doorway to victory, the final act in the defeat of Satan. Satan ruled through sickness and hunger, but his final weapon was death. And Jesus, in his resurrection, gave evidence of his own superiority, Indeed the strong man had been bound.

Jesus' victory over death and all evil powers is the explosive content of the gospel that sounded through a despairing world and radically altered subsequent human history.

Two thousand years of Christian history has often romanticized and fictionalized the status of the earliest followers of Jesus. We depict them as dramatic men of great stature, men cut from different cloth than ourselves, conquering heroes who walked with their feet three inches above the ground. We often speak of St. Peter in such awed tones that we give the impression that every time he opened his mouth to speak 10,000 angels in the background were humming the Hallelujah chorus! Simon Peter was no giant. He was a manic-depressive, waterfront rabble, a nobody, a little man. Every time he opened his mouth he stuck his foot into it up to the kneecap. Simple Simon the fisherman, he calls to Jesus asking to walk on the water. And Jesus bids him come. Then this impulsive man ventures forward in faith and steps on the water—and realizes what he has done. That is when he got his nickname, Peter the rock. He sank like a stone! Up and down, unpredictable, it is he who cries out one moment, "Even if I must die with you I will never betray you!" and minutes later he is cursing Jesus saying, "I know not the man!" This same Peter impulsively blurts out the classic foolish line of Pentecost. The church has just received the Holy Spirit. Overwhelmed, ecstatic, there are emotional overtones, and the mockers look at the disciples and conclude they are drunk. And good Peter cries out, in effect, "No, they are not drunk! It is too early in the day!" implying of course, that the church might be drunk at 5 P.M. but certainly not in the middle of the morning!

Such people Jesus gathered around him. Not heroes or giants on the face of the earth. Little people, lonely people, waterfront ruffians, hooligans, riffraff. James and John, two hothead brothers. Passing through a Samaritan village, the Samaritans would not let them pass—and their solution? To have Jesus allow them to call down a little lightning from heaven and destroy the Samaritans. And Jesus must rebuke them, calling them hotheads, *"Boanerges!* Sons of thunder!" Mary Magdalene, ex-prostitute, Zacchaeus, crippled and dwarfed tax-collector, despised by his own people. Jesus takes these nobodies and transforms them into a conquering army, the most magnificent band of revolutionaries who ever marched. Caesar crucified Jesus, but long after the echo of the tramping troops of Caesar had died away in history the armies of Jesus Christ were still marching, still conquering, still transforming human history, still reaching down into the sewers of society and with the mud they dredged up molding new men of steel and women of power.

Emmaus—and Understanding

What was it that was able to refashion human nature so dramatically and accomplish so much? How could Simple Simon become a rock indeed? John a hothead become the apostle of love? What force, what power, accomplished this?

The New Testament gives its answer: it was the

resurrection. The staggering realization, the explosive insistence, that not even death was able to overwhelm Jesus.

The Emmaus story, Luke 24:13f., capsulizes this dramatic transformation, this contagious power of the resurrection. There they are, two of them, returning home. Discouraged, broken, despairing men, trudging back to the toils of the past. And as they walk Jesus comes to them, but at first they do not recognize him. And he speaks to them, asking them why they are so sad. Their sharp answer comes back with a savagery, concealed in translation, of bitter disappointment. They had left fathers, families, fishing nets and friends. They had given up everything to follow Jesus, and now he had been crucified three days before. And with every drop of blood that trickled down the reddened post on Calvary there oozed away all their hopes and all their dreams. There was nothing left to do now but to go back to the hollow pursuits of the past as tired, discouraged, broken men. And then Jesus reveals himself to them. The power of the resurrection is made known to them. Death has been vanquished! And they race back to Jerusalem to speak of how their hearts burned within them!

In his second volume, The Acts of the Apostles, Luke continues this same theme. He calls the early preachers of the gospel, in Greek, "world-turners-upside-downers!" Men who turned the world upside down! Little men, lonely men, suddenly transformed by the power of the resurrection, throbbing through them the conviction that not even death was able to conquer Jesus. Death had lost its victory, the grave had lost its sting. They had seen a miracle! The empty tomb of the Risen Lord was large enough to hold all of their problems.

The One Who Conquers Death

Certainly, it is true, the resurrection of Jesus did not end death. There are no raptures in the early church. Certainly, it is true, the resurrection of Jesus did not end the tyranny and malignant efforts of Satan. Untold, unfair tragedy and pain continue to exist. The resurrection of Jesus was not the end of the war. It was the turning point of the war. The end would not come until the return of Jesus, when the devil was fully and finally destroyed. But it *was* the turning point! It was the historical proof that the devil had done his worst and been unsuccessful, unable to hold Jesus. "But in fact Christ has been raised from the dead!" The war went on, the enemy still waxed, and waxes, strong. But now there is nothing to fear. His impotence has been revealed. The superiority of Jesus has been affirmed. The war goes on. Men continue to fall. But even as Jesus was raised, so also shall they be raised. That is the explosive power of the gospel! The resurrection of Jesus does not tell us that Satan's reign is now ended, but it assures us that he is doomed. His immediate victories will not endure, Christ is conqueror, his will is done on earth as it is in heaven!

This explains why there can be such a juxtaposition of sentences in such places as Romans 7 and 8. In Romans 7 the apostle Paul grimly acknowledges that satanic powers still exist, that man is helpless, often overwhelmed. He can acknowledge, "I can will what is right, but I cannot do it" (Rom. 7:18). He can acknowledge that he is a wretched man with a war waging within him (Rom. 7:23-24). But he can proceed from those words, with no pessimism, with no despair, to one of those most triumphant shouts of victory in the entire New Testament. He asks the question, in the light of the powerful forces arrayed against us, "What then shall we say to this?

. . . Who shall separate us from the love of God? Shall tribulation, or distress, or persecution, or famine, or nakedness, or peril, or sword? . . . No, in all these things we are more than conquerors through him who loved us. For I am sure that neither death . . . nor anything else in all of creation will be able to separate us from the love of God in Christ Jesus our Lord" (Rom. 8:31-39).

Satan is strong. But Christ is stronger. That is why the message of Jesus can be summarized in the words he spoke so often, "Fear not!"

CONCLUSION

Proclaiming God's Victory

We have tried to show two things. First, that the New Testament believes in Satan. It takes the powers of the demonic seriously. Indeed, the entire fabric of the ministry and message of Jesus fails to make sense unless we too take Satan seriously. He is a malignant foe of great dimension. The entire ministry of Jesus unfolds against the backdrop of conflict with the evil one. And that power of Satan continues today. The resurrection was not the end of the reign of the evil one, but rather the turning point in that war. He will not be fully destroyed until the return of Jesus. The New Testament takes seriously the reality of Satan equipped with great power.

Second, we have tried to show that the New Testament is positive, optimistic, throbbing with a sense of triumph. While Satan is strong, Christ is stronger. *That* is the vibrant center of Christian thought.

And precisely at that point much contemporary religious thought, with its heavy concentration on Satan, ceases to be biblical. Contemporary thought is wrong not because, as was the case ten or fifteen years ago, it makes too little of Satan. It is wrong because it makes too much of him. Contemporary thought presents him as if he, not Jesus, is the superior one. The sense of victory is gone. The preoccupation with the demonic is not a reflection of the robust New Testament proclamation of victory. It is instead the pessimistic mirroring of our own frustration and despair. If a past generation made too little of Satan, our sin is that we make too much of him, and lose our confidence in the biblical proclamation of the victory of Jesus.

And in its morbid preoccupation with Satan today, much contemporary thought wanders into yet other areas of error. In the first place, this suffocating sense of concern with Satan today assumes that Satan is ever the same, always appearing in the same forms. In Jesus' day, demon possession meant that the victim foamed at the mouth, screamed out obscenities, rolled in the fire, and beat himself with a chain. The pictures of the demoniacs in the gospel stories are looked upon as definitive for all time. We look for the devil to act today precisely the way he did 2000 years ago. We assume that demon possession will manifest itself today just as it did in Jesus' day. We assume that the devil does not change, that his pattern of yesteryear is the same today. We fail to read what the Scripture says, that the devil can disguise himself and even take on the form of an angel of light.

The devil is not locked into one pattern for all time. He takes diverse forms, different disguises, in every age. One of Satan's greatest tricks or triumphs today is that he leads us into looking for him in precisely the same forms that he took in the past. As we run around in little circles looking for demons seeking to find in our society exact parallels with the demon-possessed of Jesus' time, we are perhaps being tricked. If we look for literal reproductions of biblical demon possession, if we assume that is where the devil is to be found, we will fail to see him in other areas where he is far more active. Surely anyone with eyes in his head must recognize that the demonic takes new and altered forms. For example, the widespread abuse of drugs today with armies of young people shattering their brains, burning up their minds, strewing the barren landscape of human existence with wasted potential and lost futures is one of Satan's areas of attack.

When we look for the devil to limit himself to only the forms he assumed in Jesus' day, we are apt to miss him where he is far more active! Drugs, Watergate, Southeast Asia, starvation in Ethiopia, unending conflict in the Middle East are some of the areas where Satan is working his malignant will in our day. But if we seek him only in explicit demon possession cases we are deeply in danger for we have not only underestimated his power, limited him to past forms, but we have also failed to recognize the larger extent of his activity in our time. That is one way in which the demonism of our day is mistaken. It gives a too small compass to the ravages of the evil one.

And the second way in which contemporary society is wrong is that whenever it talks of the devil or demons it paints the evil one in lurid ugly colors. That is a great mistake of our time, perhaps most keenly shown in the movie "The Exorcist." There the devil, the powers of darkness, are ugly, evil, destructive, repulsive, devastating. The little girl, devil-possessed, turns ugly to the extreme in her vomiting and cursing.

If the devil were that obvious he would be no problem. If all that happened when one is associated with Satan is that one merely vomited, the devil would be no problem. If evil was that obvious, and that destructive and ugly, who would associate with it? This modern preoccupation with the devil is blinding itself to the staggering scope of satanic power by making it too ugly. Satan is subtle, and evil is attractive. Not ugly but attractive. It is only when we are into it, only when we are enslaved by it, only after the fact, never in advance, that we see the ugly, destructive, devastating side of Satan. From the outside, evil is attractive, luring, enticing, promising much. By depicting it from the outset as evil and ugly we hypnotize ourselves, anesthesize ourselves and fall victim.

The ancients did not make that silly mistake. They saw the enticing luring attractive nature of the powers of darkness! Adam looked at the fruit on the tree and it looked good in his eyes. Odysseus, sailing the homeric seas, yearned to hear the sirens sing. He had his men stuff wax in their ears so they could hear nothing, but for himself, he kept his ears unstopped. He wanted to hear. Lashed to the mast, he ordered the men not to release him. And he heard the sirens sing. He wrestled with the ropes, he struggled to get free, he wanted to yield to the siren song not because it was ugly, but because it was beautiful, promising much. Only after he was smashed on the rocks would he have seen the ugly aspect of evil.

Evil has always been attractive, never ugly. That is why it entices so many. Surely the modern drug addict, glazed eyes, hollow hopes, dashed future, did not at the outset intend to prostitute his potential and shatter his life. It was not at the outset his desire

Proclaiming God's Victory

to sit staring vacantly at a blank wall seeing visions of demons in his inner eye. No addicted youngster would have become involved if at the beginning he could have foreseen the result. Drugs did not appear ugly at first. They appeared good, promising, holding out the hope of an expanded mind, an exhilarating vision of goodness. It was only after the pact had been made that the savagery of drugs exploded, carrying away all hope in the tidal wave of dehumanization.

We talk much today about Satan, but in the very talking we make the mistake of holding him in too low an esteem. We limit him to archaic forms of the past, and we mistakenly assume that he reveals from the outset the tragedy of identification with him. We camouflage his cancer and fall victim to his power.

But our greatest tragedy is that even as we speak of his strength, we fail to go the second step with the New Testament and hymn triumphantly the superiority of Jesus.

Our modern society has been stripped of the easy optimism of the past. Our society has been confronted with the problem of satanic power. Our real tragedy, however, is that while we see the problem, we fail to take seriously the promise, the answer, the assurance that there is nothing in all creation to fear, for we, with Christ, are more than conquerors. Fear not!

Our task as Christians today is not to reinforce or simply echo secular society's morbid preoccupation with satanic power, but to stride forward vigorously into the mainstream of our time with the transforming shout of victory, the good news of the gospel which is the announcement that Jesus Christ is stronger than sin, death, and the devil.

Printed in the United States
63369LVS00001B/16-63